VISUAL Literacy

Learn to See, See to Learn

Lynell Burmark

ASCD

Association for Supervision and Curriculum Development
Alexandria, Virginia USA

Association for Supervision and Curriculum Development
1703 N. Beauregard St. • Alexandria, VA 22311-1714 USA
Telephone: 1-800-933-2723 or 703-578-9600 • Fax: 703-575-5400
Web site: http://www.ascd.org • E-mail: member@ascd.org

All Web links in this book are correct as of the publication date below but may
have become inactive or otherwise modified since that time. If you notice a
deactivated or changed link, please e-mail books@ascd.org with the words
"Link Update" in the subject line. In your message, please specify the Web link
and the book title.

Printed in the United States of America.

February 2002 member book (p). ASCD Premium, Comprehensive, and
Regular members periodically receive ASCD books as part of their membership
benefits. No. FY02-05.

ASCD Product No. 101226
ASCD member price: $18.95   nonmember price: $22.95

Library of Congress Cataloging-in-Publication Data

Burmark, Lynell, 1946-
   Visual literacy : learn to see, see to learn / Lynell Burmark.
      p. cm.
Includes bibliographical references and index.
"ASCD product no. 101226"—T.p. verso.
   ISBN 0-87120-640-4 (alk. paper)
   1. Visual literacy—United States. 2. Visual learning—United
States. I. Title.
   LB1068 .B87 2002
      370.15'23—dc21   2001008367

11 10 09 08 07 06 05 04 03 02   10 9 8 7 6 5 4 3 2 1

VISUAL LITERACY
LEARN TO SEE, SEE TO LEARN

◗ Preface

MILLIONS OF WORDS HAVE BEEN PUBLISHED ON THE NEED TO increase verbal literacy in our society—that is, the need to teach people to read and write. Precious little is ever said, however, about the need for visual literacy, which is to images what reading and writing are to words. Mentioned even less is the need for teachers at all levels to learn about the basics of visual literacy, then discover how to pass that knowledge on to their students.

This void in the public discourse isn't surprising, because most people—adults and children alike—tend to believe they are already visually literate. To be sure, if you explained to average 13-year-olds what visual literacy is, they would probably assume that, like everything else, it's a skill they have already mastered. After all, they've been watching television since they were infants, seen hundreds of movies, played thousands of video and computer games, and have been continually bombarded with images and media of all kinds since the moment they were born. By now they should be experts, right?

Wrong.

Just as one does not learn to write by reading, or learn to play the guitar by listening to the radio, one does not become visually literate by simply looking at images.

Visual literacy is a learned skill, not an intuitive one. It doesn't just "happen." One becomes visually literate by studying the techniques used to create images, learning the vocabulary of shapes and colors, identifying the characteristics of an image that give it meaning, and developing the cognitive skills necessary to interpret or create the ideas that inform an image, be it a television show, photograph, painting, chart, graph, advertisement, PowerPoint slide, animated GIF, or monster movie. It takes work, study, and practice.

The process of becoming visually literate is not unlike the process of learning to read. When a child first looks at words on a page, the letters and spaces are meaningless. They appear to be nothing but random shapes—little curves and lines that big people keep pointing at all the time. In time, the child begins to associate those shapes with the sounds coming out of the parents' mouths, and is soon able to crack the mysterious code of meaning behind the words on the page. Verbal literacy involves a person's ability to interpret and use spoken and written language—to decode the world of words. Likewise, visual literacy relates to a person's ability to interpret and create visual information—to understand images of all kinds and use them to communicate more effectively.

The hidden challenge of teaching visual literacy is in convincing students that it is an important skill to learn, above and beyond one's ability to understand all the jokes in *The Simpsons*. Students need to recognize that attaining visual literacy is the necessary first step in acquiring visual intelligence, which is essential for any sort of critical thinking in the 21st century. "Seeing is believing" goes the old saying, but this axiom has never been less true than it is today. We live in an age where photos, video, and film can be digitally altered to represent any reality imaginable; an era in which what we see is *not* what we get—what we see is what the person creating the image wants us to see. True representations of the real world are rarer than ever, so it has never been more important to acquire the intellectual skills necessary to distinguish between visual fact and fiction, information and manipulation, reporting and propaganda.

Visual literacy is also an important skill to have in the professional world, where people are using many tools of digital imaging—DV camcorders, digital cameras, scanners, computers, projectors—as ordinary means of communication. In today's business world, particularly in the areas of marketing, publishing, advertising and graphic design, a lack of visual literacy is as much a handicap as the inability to read or write. The fields of engineering, medicine, law, journalism, sales, and politics—to say

nothing of the arts and entertainment industries—are also becoming increasingly sophisticated in their use of modern imaging technologies, and are therefore in need of people who can understand and use these technologies.

The student who does not see the value in visual literacy simply isn't looking in the right place. That's why this book is so important. For many, it will represent a vital first step toward learning skills of perception and judgment that will pay dividends over a lifetime. If you're lucky and work hard, this book may even allow you to see the world with fresh eyes, which is a gift that doesn't come often in this life. Together, verbal and visual literacy are the cornerstones of communication in the 21st century. Students who master them will go far, and perhaps see even farther.

—Tad Simons
Editor-in-Chief, *Presentations* Magazine

▶ Foreword

IN HER YEARS AS AN ASSOCIATE OF THE THORNBURG CENTER, Lynell Burmark has earned a solid reputation as an expert in visual communications. Her landmark workshop "Strategies for Successful Presentations" has become a favorite with people who have to stand up and inform an audience with multimedia.

But it's not razzle-dazzle that earns the author her high regard. She can use compelling imagery with the best of them; but, far more important, she knows what the images do to people and how to use them conscientiously and appropriately for the purpose at hand. She knows, too, how to teach other people these same skills, and that is the purpose of this excellent book. You will rarely have such a good time learning so much.

▶ ▶ ▶

Why should you care about visual literacy? Ask yourself this question: If you had to leave your home in a hurry, and all family members and pets were safely outside, what one thing would you take with you? If you are like most people, you'd say, "My photos." Pictures you've taken over the years are probably valuable to you because a picture is worth far more than a thousand words. In fact, you can't compare pictures with words at all. Pictures represent information in far different ways than words, and they communicate completely differently.

As Burmark clearly shows, visual literacy is different from the literacy associated with the world of words.

Television and the World Wide Web are but two of the myriad places today where images carry content with visceral power. Images convey emotions and facts simultaneously. The effect of an image is virtually instantaneous, and the viewer responds without conscious thought. Our youth have become sophisticated viewers of images and are learning how to use images themselves as a powerful method of communicating ideas. The challenge is that this skill is often not refined, and that many educators lack the basic visual literacy needed to guide and evaluate student productions, let alone communicate effectively with their own audiences.

This comes home to me most obviously at academic conferences where intelligent researchers manage to strip every shred of excitement or enthusiasm from their work by using presentation tools limited to black-and-white overhead transparencies of their purely text-based handouts. Even when these folks make the move to computer-based presentations, they still often fall back on heavily text-laden slides.

So, why would you want to read this particular book? This volume is important for several reasons. First, by exploring the topic of visual literacy in some depth, you'll come to understand why it needs to take its place alongside traditional definitions of literacy.

Second, this book will help make you a more effective communicator. In our fast-paced world, the capacity to express ideas clearly and quickly is essential. Images not only communicate rapidly, they do so with lasting effect.

Third, if you do presentations for students or peers, this book will help you. If you are working with young people, this book will help you gain familiarity with their natural way of getting information, and help you teach them how to become more effective visual communicators.

The capacity to communicate effectively has always been a hallmark of an educated person. To communicate effectively through images will be increasingly important in the coming years. By choosing this book, you've shown your desire to develop this essential skill.

—DAVID THORNBURG
DIRECTOR, THORNBURG CENTER FOR
PROFESSIONAL DEVELOPMENT

▶ Introduction

WELCOME TO THE WORLD OF IMAGES. WE'VE ALWAYS USED images to communicate—from the days of the cave paintings through the history of photography to today's visually saturated environment packed with everything from television, movies, video games, and illustrated news media to holographic photo IDs.

But somehow, today, it's different. The images have become less of a decorative element and more an integral part of the communication.

When we speak of visual literacy, we are addressing the basic "reading" (interpreting) and "writing" (producing/using) of visually imbued communications. As we take a comprehensive look at visual literacy from the K–12 classroom perspective, we examine different aspects of visual images and how both teacher- and student-generated graphics can improve communication and understanding in the classroom. We underscore the visual impact of fonts and typefaces in print, presentation, and Web-based lessons, and spell out the rules for effective use of text. We include an introductory course on color, complete with graphics and exercises for classroom use.

We visit exemplary classrooms and share their visual displays and strategic use of visuals in a range of subject areas. We link visual expression and technology—sharing practical, insider tips and expertise in developing and delivering electronic presentations. In the last chapter, we have some fun in the "digital playground," demonstrating how computer and Web-based graphics can make teaching and learning more fun as well as more effective.

Busy professionals will appreciate the book's wealth of replicable ideas and activities and resources for free color images. A complementary CD-ROM is available from the author with printable lesson plans, slide shows, and projection-quality color photographs. Contact the author directly for ordering information (lynellb@aol .com).

Armed with this book and CD, not only will teachers and training professionals understand *why* instruction must be more visually based, but they will also know *what* to change and *how* to make the transformation. Along with their students, they will be equipped to master visual literacy: *the* basic skill for 21st century schools.

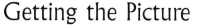

Getting the Picture

WELCOME TO THE AGE OF IMAGES. THE SIGNS ARE EVERYWHERE —for those who can read them. The primary literacy of the 21st century will be visual: pictures, graphics, images of every kind. Engineering, architecture, computer trades, health care professions, even jobs as pedestrian as cooking fries at McDonald's (now done with sophisticated robotics) all require visual literacy. It's no longer enough to be able to read and write. Our students must learn to process both words *and* pictures. They must be able to move gracefully and fluently between text and images, between literal and figurative worlds.

This is the day of a new kind of visionary, one who imbues the term with a powerful new meaning. The saying "What you see is what you get" today has a vast new significance, because what you get from what you see is shaped by a profound new consciousness of images and how to process them. If you can't quite picture how this came to be, let's look at a snapshot summary of some significant history and see how we got here.

Snapshot History of Visual Imagery

Pictures were once relatively rare. People just didn't have that much access to them. For millennia if you wanted to see a painting, you had to be in a cave or one of a small number of rooms dedicated to art. Photography isn't two centuries old yet, and in its first century very few people saw prints. The era of ubiquitous imagery began with the ubiquitous usage of electricity, barely the blink of an eye ago.

In December 1895 the Lumière brothers in France gave the first public viewing of a motion picture at a café in Paris, followed in April 1896 by Edison's Vitascope projection at Koster & Bial's Music Hall (now Macy's) in New York City.[1] Fifty years later, in 1946, half the population of the United States went to the movies at least once a week.[2]

That same year, limited broadcasting began of a hot new technology—television. Suddenly pictures were everywhere, evidenced by a proliferation of visually oriented publications such as *Life*; the photo magazine *Roto*

Gravure was so well known it earned a reference in Irving Berlin's classic song "Easter Parade." In the early '80s came *USA Today* and the rise of more graphically oriented newspapers such as *The St. Louis Post-Dispatch* and *The Washington Times*. For several years these three papers jockeyed for top spot in industry art awards. Despite much hand wringing over a potential blow to in-depth journalism, these dailies pioneered the development of a new, visual erudition. Then came computers, video games, and the rest of the toys of today that fuel the New Economy.

Got the picture?

The age of images ushered in more than just still and moving photographs. It brought with it a heightened awareness of the language of visuals, a form of speech that goes beyond the nuances of words to the insinuations of images. How we interpret those insinuations has been largely shaped by how publishers, producers, broadcasters, designers, and artists have delivered images.

Film director Haskell Werner asserted that the age of images was wrought almost single-handedly by television. Werner directed *Medium Cool*, a film that addressed the quality of motion pictures as being a "cool" medium, by which he meant it had a certain aloofness from the viewer that allowed a greater visual impact. "Television brought about a distinct acuity of imagery in viewers," he said.[3] It could hardly be otherwise. The United States is indeed a nation of avid television watchers (see illustration), and the younger the viewer, the more television watched. A 1994 study by Yale University reported that the average U.S. elementary school student watched between 5 and 6 hours of television a day. Children in poverty watched as much as 7 hours. By the time a student graduated from high school, he had logged some 22,000 hours of television.[4]

And "the tube" is not just an American phenomenon. An aerial shot of the slums of Rio de Janeiro, for example, reveals so many satellite dishes that the area resembles a field of mushrooms. Small wonder that children around the world are increasingly visually oriented in their learning.

Contemporary students' learning styles are further shaped not just by the technology they view, but also by the nature of the programming. Consider the length of common entertainment forms. The average movie used to be about two hours long; today it's closer to 90 minutes. Early television programs were commonly an hour or longer and were typically just photographed versions of stage acts. Today 60 minutes is still a common program length, but the omnipresent situation comedy (sitcom), in which the story resolves varied intertwining elements of action and situations in an amazingly brief period of time, is rarely longer than a half hour. TV programs have increasingly condensed attention and scope of content. And TV and other media have increasingly interwoven visuals and the meaning of words, dialogue, and narration.

Visuals in Instruction

It's time for teachers to take advantage of the way kids entertain themselves today, to employ those same media and the thinking habits they foster for the betterment of student learning. To do so not only allows another way to reach children, but also stretches us into a greater understanding of how the human mind so wonderfully adapts to and integrates new tools. The child born into poverty will be even more affected by visual influences than more advantaged classmates. (Ask any inner-city school to conduct a survey of the students' homes and compare the number of books to the number of televisions.) There is opportunity here. The child who watches multiple lines of thought and action conflicting, interacting, and often resolving themselves in less than half an hour on the screen may find that those vicarious experiences engender perception, insight, and problem-solving confidence applicable to real-life situations. Because so much of students' experience is shaped and surrounded by imagery, visual literacy truly has become the new currency of learning.

Visual Literacy—What Is it?
Why Is It Important?

What exactly does it mean to be visually literate? Experts offer differing opinions on this relatively recent area of study. In his presentation at the 1996 International Visual Literacy Association Conference, Jerry Christopherson said that a visually literate person should be able to

- Interpret, understand, and appreciate the meaning of visual messages;

- Communicate more effectively by applying the basic principles and concepts of visual design;

- Produce visual messages using computers and other technologies; and

- Use visual thinking to conceptualize solutions to problems.[5]

These skills are increasingly important for students today, both for learning and for workplace preparation. Many papers presented at International Visual Literacy Association conferences document a firm correlation between visual literacy and overall intelligence and performance in technical content areas. As the use of technology and computers increases, so will the need to create and communicate through visual images. But there are other, less obvious, perhaps even more significant factors that mandate the use of visual teaching.

Visual literacy becomes a powerful teaching ally in classrooms where not all students speak the same language. In many schools in the United States, especially in states like California, Texas, and Florida, more and more students speak English as a *second* language. In these situations, visuals become a kind of international, universal language that brings meaning to an otherwise incomprehensible cacophony of verbal expression. California's teachers, in particular, must rely heavily on the use of visuals for this purpose: The state now has a law requiring all classes to be taught only in English after the first 30 days of school.

Many children in U.S. schools today have emigrated from war-torn and economically ravaged countries. These children often use visual images to communicate and process the trauma of their young lives. Even for American-born children, the culture has changed to a new order. The days of *Ozzie and Harriet* and *Leave It to*

Beaver families where *Father Knows Best* are no longer the norm in schools where too many fathers have deserted the family, have been killed, or are in prison. No longer can teachers assume their students are bringing a homogenous set of experiences with them when they enter school. More and more children arrive in kindergarten never having been read to, not knowing how to hold a book, unaware of what to do with the letters that could spell their own names. Although the average child in the United States has had approximately 3,000 hours of pre-school language literacy experience at home before entering the 1st grade, the ever-growing population of at-risk children averages only 260 hours of such experience.[6] The longer a child is left failing, the more difficult remediation becomes. Without serious intervention, poor readers in 1st grade will still not be reading at grade level in 4th grade. For all too many youths, that illiteracy spells disaster for life. The Indiana state prison system is so convinced of the correlation that it calculates future needs for prison beds by considering the number of children failing reading in the primary grades.[7]

Clearly, when students graduate from high school, they need to be reading fluently. More and more, the good jobs also require technical skills, as well as the ability to work productively in teams. Employers are also looking for traits such as honesty, creativity, and willingness to take risks. The workplace landscape is changing dramatically, corresponding to the frenetic pace of technological progress.

Looking Ahead

The simple fact of the aging of the working population in the United States affects our standards of living powerfully.

Projections by the U.S. Census Bureau[8] show that the ratio of those in the 18–64 age group to those 65 and older will decline from 4.8 in 1995 to 2.8 in 2050. The Department of Commerce[9] concludes that demand will increase over time for a work force with essential science, technology, and engineering competencies. The Commerce Department study states:

> Given this trend, the productivity per worker must increase to maintain or increase the average standard of living. Without productivity increases, some economic changes (e.g., inflation or a declining stock market) could lead to a decline in living standards for almost all Americans, including those who have put aside what should have been adequate retirement funds.

The study also points out that over the last half-century, the fields of science, technology, and engineering have accounted for more than half of the nation's productivity increases.

Some of that productivity has come at the cost of work that pretty much anybody could once do. Corporate America is very concerned about the quality of worker it will receive in coming years. The workplace study group, Council on Competitiveness, calls worker skills the greatest competitive challenge the United States faces over the next decade. Its report *Winning the Skills Race* states that the demand for increased skills is rising much faster than the capacity of U.S. companies or the education system to respond.[10]

A Department of Labor report[11] reveals that many jobs previously done by unskilled and low-skilled workers are now handled through sophisticated automated machines. Today, workers are expected to perform tasks of increased complexity. "For example," the report says, "sales clerks may no longer need to key in the price of an item, but can either scan the product or *point to a picture of the item*" (emphasis added). The globalization of production further alters the skill requirements of U.S. workers. Moving more jobs abroad in search of cheaper low-skilled labor decreases the demand for such workers in the United States, while increasing the need for higher-skilled Americans who supervise foreign production.[12] And as more Americans work with people from other countries, the need for vehicles of common communication, notably visuals, increases.

On an individual level, skill in the marketplace increasingly draws on visual literacy. Research by 3M Corporation[13] shows that people are able to process visual information 60,000 times more quickly than textual information. Business today uses that fact constantly and to dramatic advantage. A study conducted by 3M and *Presentations* magazine[14] asked participants to choose between two hypothetical banks with identical fees and services based on how banking information was presented to them. Although absolutely no differences existed between the two banks, 79 percent of the participants chose the bank that delivered its information by an enhanced multimedia presentation. That bank, they said, was more credible, more professional, and offered better services and fees. In the same issue, *Presentations* concluded that "visual learners don't learn from words on a screen, but from simple, bold images."[15] This also explains why presentations that feature text-heavy slides—still all too common in both business and education—are ironically self-defeating. Business is increasingly aggressive about using the power of visuals in presentations, Web, and print-based communications.[16] Education generally is behind the curve.

Silicon Valley corporate leaders are bemoaning the demands of what they call the new "attention economy,"[17] in which the time allowed to engage interest grows shorter and shorter. Newspaper surveys throughout the '70s and '80s concluded that print material had an average of 13 seconds in which to capture attention; thresholds of interest had to be reached quickly, and the first, most critical threshold was visual interest. Few people could be bothered to read something if it didn't look immediately inviting. When the elements of that visual threshold were analyzed, it was shown that there were clear factors in graphical representation that held the eye (and, conversely, clear factors that caused the eye to quickly move on). Similar thresholds exist in electronic media. Television programming strives to hold the attention of the channel surfer. Web designers try to create "sticky" sites where visitors will stay long enough to make purchases online. Web design guru Jakob Nielsen warns against overly long download times because "10 seconds [is] the maximum response time before users lose interest. On the Web, users have been trained to endure so much suffering that it may be acceptable to increase this limit to 15 seconds for a few pages."[18] An entire new industry has been spawned to cure the "world wide wait." At a recent Internet Commerce Expo in Boston, Fireclick's Blueflame software was selected from 150 contenders to win "Best of Show" because of its outstanding ability to speed Web access for online consumers.[19]

What does this mean for classroom instruction? How can teachers who assumed they had 12 years to teach something suddenly develop expertise in delivering pithy sound bytes, compelling and "sticky" instruction?

Short of recruiting teachers from the ranks of MTV stars and Las Vegas stand-up comedians, how does education vie for students' attention? Traditional instructional practices simply can't compete on that level. Where educators have the advantage—and the opportunity—is in involving students in the production, in making them the stars. If the classroom becomes a learning stage, where the teachers become the audience and the critic, and the students assume the roles of playwrights, actors, set designers, lighting crew, and so forth, students will learn to think imaginatively, and they will become excited about learning.

Rather than teaching to the test, which stresses teachers and demoralizes students, schools can adopt an arts-integrated education system where teachers are energized and students are empowered across the curriculum. Many schools are reporting that successes in art, music, and drama "transfer" to better scores on standardized tests of basic skills. Words and images—the synergy is irrefutable. And the payoff is lifelong.

Here's Looking at You

LET'S START THIS CHAPTER BY TESTING YOUR VISUAL PERCEPTION skills. Do you think the two women in the picture are

a) Reacting to the news that they may have just won a million dollars?
b) Just returning from the dentist and want to show off their new choppers?

c) Watching reruns of the 2000 U.S. presidential election returns? or
d) Trying on a new line of berets and wedding veils?

Your guess is as good as anyone else's, of course, but the point is that it is only a guess. Unless you were there, you would not know the story behind the picture. A more telling point, and the heart of this chapter's message, is that every picture does indeed have a story behind it. This is true for visuals in our family photo albums, as well as for those symbols and images imbued with socially recognized significance that bombard us every day. They are visual mnemonics—memories of life experiences and feelings recaptured through nonverbal means.

I'll explain the funny, touching story behind this photograph at the end of this chapter. For the moment, I will say that it holds many memories for me.

Good teachers have always known that visual images help learners understand and remember complex infor-mation and abstract concepts. In 400 B.C.E. (Before the Christian Era), in the *Phaedo*, Plato recounts Socrates describing two worlds: the murky, tangled world of speech versus the perfect, well-lit world of imagery. In 1658, pansophist philosopher John Amos Comenius pub-lished *The Visible World*, considered to be one of the first illustrated books for children. Both Freud and Piaget rec-ognized that young children handle concrete images more easily than abstract words.

Verbal or Visual?

Pundits and philosophers continue to debate the relative importance of verbal and visual systems of communica-tion. Umberto Eco declares that language is what constitutes human beings. He goes on to say that next to verbal language, all other languages are imperfect approximations.[1] Those who share this view of the primacy of verbal communication often fear that the a preponderance of visual communication will lead to the degeneration of language. In doomsday books like *Technopoly*[2] and *The End of Education*,[3] Neil Postman blames most of the world's problems on the switch from books to television. In October 1999 Geoffrey Meredith proclaimed in *The Futurist*: "Text is toast." Meredith further elaborated:

> In 100 years, few people will want to read at all, and fewer still will know how to write. Text will be outmoded, except for instruction booklets and the aptly named textbooks containing technical information.
>
> Communication, both factual and expressive, will be through sound and pictures. We will have returned to the troubadour, the cave painter, the oral tradition, and come full circle back to the age of Homer.[4]

Though it might be easy to dismiss Meredith's and Postman's perceptions as paranoia, some of their concerns may be well founded. According to *Time* magazine, for example, the vocabulary of the average 14-year-old dropped from 25,000 words in 1950 to only 10,000 words by 1999.[5] According to *Newsweek* magazine, 22 percent of college students would rather pick up trash on campus than write a paper; 47 percent would rather donate blood.[6]

Rather than envisioning a downward spiral where images destroy words, I prefer to think we can find a way to make the two communication systems work symbiotically. I believe that it is through the combination of words and images that we elevate our thinking to the highest levels of understanding.

Our Words Versus *Their* Images: The Importance of Context

As educators, we need to help students verbalize their dreams. If we start with *our* words—spelling lists, vocabulary lists, blocks of black text on white pages, or swirls of white chalk on blackboards—we may or may not connect to *their* images and life experiences. Remember the vocabulary-building exercises in the *Reader's Digest* magazine? Very few students (or adults for that matter) would turn off the television to spend time matching those words to definitions. But is it the distaste for words or the decontextualized nature of the exercise that makes the task relatively boring? What about the lyrics to a popular song? Do you hear students complaining about the latest pop singer repeating the same words over and over? Again, the context of the music raises both communication systems (words and music) to a higher plane.

A look at recent brain research puts this discussion in a more academic context and sheds light on the importance of images as they work synergistically with words, music, motion, and other mental processing channels.

The Research Perspective

Gardner's Theory of Multiple Intelligences

For most educators, the most accessible and compelling brain research has come from Howard Gardner, Co-Director of Project Zero at the Harvard Graduate School of Education, and Adjunct Professor of Neurology at the Boston University of Medicine. With his brilliant conception of individual competence, Gardner has reframed educational policy and practice. Educators first "discovered"

Gardner when he published his seminal work, *Frames of Mind*, in 1983.[7] Thousands of teachers, as well as parents and educational researchers, embraced the concepts that

- The human brain houses separate capacities or "intelligences."
- Each child's intelligence is actually a unique combination of these "multiple intelligences."

According to Gardner, while most people possess at least eight intelligences, traditional educational practice has focused on only three (see first table). Most of us learn better when additional intelligences are involved (see second table).

①	Linguistic	Words
②	Logical–Mathematical	Numbers
③	Intrapersonal	Self

④	Interpersonal	Others
⑤	Spatial/Visual	Pictures
⑥	Musical	Music
⑦	Bodily Kinesthetic	Body
⑧	Naturalist	Nature

The real power comes from the synergy of combining multiple intelligences. Research confirms what educators had already known intuitively and reinforced experien-

tially: Combining visual images with written text can help students remember what they read.

Pavio's Processing

Allan Pavio echoes Gardner's theory when he postulates that visual and verbal information are encoded and decoded by separate, specialized perceptual and cognitive channels in the brain. The visual channel manipulates image elements simultaneously; the linguistic channel functions in a linear, sequential manner. When the same information is presented to the brain in different forms (i.e., verbal and visual) Pavio calls it "dual coding." Pavio's theory is that the brain involves independent yet interdependent systems so concepts can flow seamlessly between their linguistic labels and their visual representations.[8]

In "Teaching Visual Literacy in a Multimedia Age," Glenda Rakes reviews more evidence to support Pavio's dual coding theory:

Using positron emission tomography (PET scans), medical researchers have been able to demonstrate that different areas of the brain become active when individuals are exposed to verbal and visual information. When individuals were asked to look at and remember verbal information, two regions in the brain's verbal domain—the left hemisphere—became active. When presented with visual information, the right hemisphere lit up.

Given this information, the use of visuals in instructional materials takes on a larger dimension than when simply thought of as decorative supplements to text. The use of visuals with text can provide that dual code that can, in turn, increase comprehension.[9]

Illustrated Texts

In a 1982 study, Levie and Lentz reported findings from 55 experiments comparing learning from illustrated text versus text alone. They noted that illustrations contributed to reader interest and enjoyment, affected attitudes and emotions, and provided spatial information that was difficult to express in words. They also calculated that groups using illustrated texts performed 36 percent better than groups using text alone on measured criteria.[10]

Visual Thinking

Robert L. Lindstrom, author of *The Business Week Guide to Multimedia Presentations*, explains the physiological basis of "visual thinking":

> Of all our sense receptors, the eyes are the most powerful information conduit to the brain. They send information to the cerebral cortex through two optic nerves, each consisting of 1,000,000 nerve fibers. By comparison, each auditory nerve consists of a mere 30,000 fibers.
>
> Nerve cells devoted to visual processing . . . account for about 30% of the brain's cortex, compared to 8% for touch and 3% for hearing.
>
> With all the bandwidth to the brain, it's no wonder we perceive the world and communicate in visual terms. We read fives times as fast as the average person talks. We register a full-color image, the equivalent of a megabyte of data, in a fraction of a second.[11]

Visual Aids

Not surprisingly, companies who help us produce or duplicate visual images have conducted some of the most interesting research on the power of visuals. Although they ostensibly target the business customer, their findings have enormous ramifications for instructional practice.

Did you know, for example, that visual aids have been found to improve learning by up to 400 percent?[12] This research confirms our daily experience: We rely on images to bring ideas and concepts to life.

The widely quoted 1986 study sponsored by 3M at the University of Minnesota School of Management quantified the persuasive power of presentations. It found that presenters who use visual aids are 43 percent more effective in persuading audience members to take a desired course of action than presenters who don't use visuals. Presenters of various skill levels attempted to persuade undergraduate students to commit time and money to attending seminars on time management. The researchers observed that average presenters using visual aids were rated "better" than presenters using no visuals. The study also revealed that the audience *expected* better presenters to use high-quality visual support.[13]

Another interesting aspect of the 1986 study was that audience comprehension and retention improved dramatically when black and white visuals were replaced with color. In a recent issue of its monthly newsletter, "Meeting Guides," 3M reviews additional research on "The Power of Color in Presentations"[14]:

- Color visuals increase willingness to read by up to 80 percent.
- Using color can increase motivation and participation by up to 80 percent.
- Color enhances learning and improves retention by more than 75 percent.
- Color accounts for 60 percent of the acceptance or rejection of an object and is a critical factor in the success of any visual experience.

- Using color in advertising outsells black and white by . . . 88 percent.

The article goes on to share what a recent customer survey of presenters using 3M overhead projectors revealed:

- 50 percent felt that using color made the presenter appear more professional.
- 77 percent agreed that "Presentations that use color are able to communicate better than those that use black and white."
- 72 percent agreed that "Presentations that use color are remembered longer than those that use black and white."

The article suggests the old children's riddle—"What's black and white and read (red) all over?"—no longer applies to our current newspapers, especially the Sunday edition with the sought-after, fought-over comics section.

I can't help but think of the teacher's version of the riddle:

"What's black and white and red (but probably not read) all over?"

Of course, the answer would be: "A corrected student worksheet."

How often, as teachers, have we spent more time correcting an assignment than the student spent doing it? Any time there's more red (teacher) ink than black (student) ink on the page, the wrong person is doing the work. (We already know the answers. Why should we write the same corrections in red 20–30 times?)

In any case, we will be discussing in great detail how color communicates in Chapter 4 of this book. We'll also be giving tips on using color in computer-based presentations in Chapter 6. In the meantime, if you haven't already, may I suggest that you take out your yellow marker? It's a great tool for highlighting the practical tips you can use in the rest of this chapter!

Precision of Images over Words

When you're trying to convey an object, using a photograph (or showing the actual object) is going to be more precise than describing it in words. In fact, at times, the words may conjure up a completely different image than the object(s) they were intended to evoke.

For example, ask a group of students to make a picture in their heads when you say "hot dog." Then show them the photo on this page and ask how many saw exactly that.

Of course, in cases where students have limited knowledge of the language of instruction, the words may not mean anything at all. (*Par example, quelle sorte d'animal auriez-vous imaginée si je vous avais demandé en français d'imaginer un chien chaud?*)

And even when they understand the words, students coming from many different backgrounds and cultures will bring different life experiences to mind. Portland artist and educator Bonnie Meltzer suggests the following experiment:[15]

On a piece of paper, draw an elephant.

Then draw a wombat or an ibex.

What is essential about the elephant? It is much easier to draw an elephant than the other two animals because elephant imagery is ubiquitous. What do we know about an elephant? You might not have drawn every detail right, but you did include the trunk, right?

Did you draw an ibex or a wombat? Why not? Ah, you didn't know what either of them looks like?

If you don't know what something looks like, you can't draw it.

If it doesn't relate or connect to something in your own experience, you can't even imagine it. Would it help if I told you the wombat was a stocky, short-legged, furry badger-like animal that measures up to four feet long and weighs 30–75 pounds? Would you like to see a picture?[16]

As for the ibex, until I checked out its picture on the Internet,[17] I thought it was a bird!

From the Concrete to the Abstract: A Rose Is a Rose...

Particularly for younger students, it is easier to process concrete objects and images rather than more abstract concepts like words and ideas. If our goal as teachers and presenters is to have everyone "on the same page," everyone seeing the same image in their mind's eye, what is the fastest and surest way to make that happen? Try this little exercise and gauge the response.

Ask the group to create a picture in their heads when you say or display the words "pink rose."

Then show them a clip art image of a pink rose[18] and ask how many saw exactly that rose.

Then show the photograph[19] of the rose you actually wanted them to imagine (see below).

Again, few people will have "seen" exactly this rose from just the words "pink rose." (Of course, to fully experience the rose, you would have the actual flower so everyone could feel its velvety petals and inhale its sweet perfume.)

Although most educators and presenters eventually realize that words may not paint unequivocal pictures, unfortunately, most do not suspect how ambiguous and ineffective clip art can be. Nor do they realize that letting students turn in clip art as part of their "original" work deprives them of the synergistic access to both sides of their brain (drawing *images* from the right side of the brain, drawing *words* from the left).

Meltzer[20] provides a helpful comparison (see table):

Use Original Artwork	Use Clip Art
Ownership of work	No ownership of work
Growth	No growth
Self-expression	No self-expression
Acceptance of child's work	Unintended criticism of child
Gain in self-confidence	No gain in confidence
Learn observation skills	No observation skills
Learn more computer skills	Learn fewer computer skills
Unique products	Canned look
Cohesive style	Possible mishmash of styles
Creative experience	Not a creative experience
Extensive decision making	Minimal decision making

In a similar manner, formula art (providing preprinted images for coloring in or cutting out) has more to do with conforming to an accepted norm than with providing children an outlet for creative expression.

In his eye-opening book, *Draw Me a Story: An Illustrated Exploration of Drawing-as-Language*, Bob Steele urges educators to recognize children's drawings for what they represent:

- Artifacts from the child's mental life.
- Products of the child's imagination.
- Attempts to make sense of the world in whatever medium is available and most easily used.[21]

Tacoma Public Schools Art teacher Monica Meeks showed me watercolors done by 3rd graders she had asked to "paint something blue." Almost every painting had blue sky over a large body of blue water with a brown blob in it. She tearfully came to realize that, for those children, their only experience with blue water was when they went to visit their fathers in prison at the McNeil Island federal penitentiary.

Another drawing, done in crayon by a 4th grader, focuses on home and family life (see illustration). Relationships among family members are weighing on this child's mind. When asked to identify the stick figures, she pointed out that she and her mother were on the left side; and her father, who travels a lot, was on the right. More deep feelings came out as the child described other elements of the picture.

I was visiting some friends one Sunday afternoon and asked their 12-year-old daughter Samantha if she would like to draw some pictures for the book I was writing. She drew this beautiful cat with a dainty little computer mouse (see illustration).

Because she is studying Japanese and currently fascinated by all things from that language and culture, she signed the drawing with her artist's name, Saiki. The meticulous detail revealed in the sketch was further demonstrated by the fact that she dated her work.

Her younger brother, Jay, never to be outdone, presented me not only with his drawing, but also the song it illustrates (see drawing, next page):

Dino Bells, Dino Bells.
Dinos everywhere!
Dinos here, Dinos there,
T-rex ate my hair.

In the crayon drawing, you see Jay's self-portrait. (He's the bald one with an exclamation point next to him.) As you might suspect, he's one of those kids who knew the name of every dinosaur by the time he was 3 years old. He prided himself on being able to spell as well as read and pronounce those names.

Elliot Eisner, professor of education and art at the Stanford University School of Education, is as fascinated as I am by what children reveal when they create a visual image. According to Eisner:

> Children leave their own personal "thumbprint" on each of the images they create. The same tree seen by different children takes on each child's distinctive mode of perception and representation. Objects that matter to them the most take on a visual significance in their work. Children tend to exaggerate those aspects of a drawing, painting, or sculpture that are most meaningful to them.[22]

Just think of the huge suns and the colorful flowers as big as houses in the drawings of happy children. How much more joy would adults experience if we could hold on to that perspective?

Humor

No discussion of the power of visual images would be complete without paying tribute to visual humor. Just as the unanticipated pairing of disparate words can create puns and spawn laughter, so the juxtaposition of images can surprise and delight us. For a class project, students can collect humorous advertisements like this magazine ad from Kinko's offering busy people a pickup and delivery service (see "daytimer" photo).

Students can dissect what makes these visual compositions funny. They can also work in teams ("advertising agencies") to develop humorous series of advertisements ("campaigns") related to a topic they are studying. Once the techniques of humor are understood, students can be challenged to draw or photograph their own humorous visual compositions for print, computer-based presentations, or Web sites.

The World Wide (Resource) Web

Where do you (and your students) go to find good photographic images? What if you really need to see what a wombat looks like and you don't have time to go looking for one in the Australian outback? Would you like millions of images categorized and delivered to your desktop computer? I keep thinking someone is going to pinch me, and I'll wake up and discover there really is no World Wide Web. But until that happens, I keep buying larger hard drives to store more "perfect images" from the Internet. In Chapters 6 and 7, I'll share dozens of my favorites with you as we see how to use photographic images in presentations and a variety of classroom projects.

To conclude this chapter on the power of images, here are a few compelling sites that underscore *how photographic images can enrich the curriculum*. What if your English class is reading a novel on the Holocaust or your history class is studying the Civil War or the fall of the Berlin Wall?

For example, what does the "Gettysburg hero" print (see photo) from the Mathew Brady collection of Civil War photographs tell you about this wounded veteran?[23]

The date was 1863. Ask your students:

- Was the war over?
- Where do you think he's sitting?
- What's leaning up against the wall? Against the doors?
- What does his posture tell you about what's in his heart?

Ask your students to download other images from the Brady collection and talk about what they see (http://memory.loc.gov/ammem/cwphtml/cwphome.html).

In Juergen Mueller-Schneck's collection of photos of the Berlin Wall (www.dieberlinermauer.de/indexenglish .html), why is the East German soldier looking so wistful as he gazes across the wall?[24] Why is the woman crying the day the wall came down?

Are your high school students reading *The Diary of Anne Frank*? Try seeing her life against the backdrop of Alan Jacobs's photos of the Holocaust (http://www .remember.org).[25]

What emotional impact do these photographs have on you? Can you relate to the people in the photos? Can you imagine being in their place? Ask students to select a photograph that touches them, and ask them to share with the class how it deepened their understanding or changed their perspective on the characters or historical events.

Many Native American and Asian cultures prohibit photography because they believe that the photographer steals their souls when he takes a picture. Sometimes it does seem that the spirit of the person has been captured, at least for that moment in time.

Ask your students to bring in portraits of friends or family members whose personality seems to jump off the paper. Ask them to describe the person in the photo— not the physical appearance, but the essence behind the outward expressions.

Encourage them to take photographs of their own family, pets, and friends and "introduce" them to the rest of the class. In the process, they just might preserve some treasured memories, as well as learn about the power of images to communicate ideas and values to other people.

My Miss Schmidt

Remember the photo at the beginning of the chapter? What did you see in the picture? In case you are curious, this photograph was taken at my wedding reception; I'm the bride in the picture. The woman with me is Miss Schmidt, my 4th grade teacher.

My mother surprised me by tracking Miss Schmidt down and inviting her to the wedding. Of all the great teachers I had over the years, Miss Schmidt was my favorite. I still remember that she would read to us every day after lunch and that she taught us songs in German.

So why were we laughing so hard in this picture? We were remembering the last time my father had met with

Miss Schmidt, when I was still her 9-year-old student and she was still unmarried. It was during one of those compulsory parent-teacher conferences. Miss Schmidt made the mistake of asking my father what he thought I would be when I grew up. His tactless reply was: "I'm afraid she's going to end up an old-maid schoolteacher." Decades later, on this blessed occasion, we were recalling that conversation and chortling that my dad was only half right. I did end up a schoolteacher, but now both Miss Schmidt and I had husbands!

Remember the Miss Schmidts in your life? I would encourage you to share pictures of these people with your students or other audiences and ask them what they see. Use the images as an illustration of an important point you want to make.

Pictures are only the islands in the sun, the visible tips of remembered experiences and feelings that plunge far below the surface. Take this funny little story of Miss Schmidt, for example. It has more depth than meets the eye:

Miss Schmidt was the first of my teachers who asked me to correct papers from the other students. All these years, I was convinced that she had picked me because I was always the first person to finish my work. It wasn't until very recently that I finally realized why she had chosen me.

Before she asked me to correct the other students' papers, Miss Schmidt had given me an answer key and asked me to correct my own paper. I was mortified to discover that I had one wrong answer. I remember thinking: "I could just change it." Then the moral dialogue commenced: "What's more important, being honest or getting 100% correct on the test?" The answer was clear, and I handed Miss Schmidt back my paper with a big, ugly red scrawl (– 1) across the top of the paper. She smiled broadly and gave me 30 more papers to correct.

I finally understood that Miss Schmidt was less interested in the quantity of my brains than the quality of my heart.

She cared more about character than intelligence. She understood that to ignite children's minds you must first touch their hearts. Obviously, she touched mine.

3 Type, "The Unconscious Persuader"[1]

You are cordially invited to attend an audit hosted in your honor by the IRS.

WHAT WAS YOUR FIRST IMPRESSION WHEN YOU SAW THIS INVITATION[2]? Did you anticipate a wedding or a formal dinner party? Were you able to decipher the swirling capital letters to realize your host would be the Internal Revenue Service?

If this were a real communication from the IRS, the typeface would not be nearly as pretty. In fact, all IRS forms are set in Helvetica—the second most commonly used typeface in the United States. We may not remember the *name* of the font family, but we do remember its (type)*face* and how it made us feel when we last saw it.

Return this voucher with check or money order payable to the "Internal Revenue Service." Please write your social security number and "2001 Form 1040-ES" on your check or money order. Do not send cash. Do not staple your payment to this voucher.

Just the request for payment in this box sends a chill up my spine. I have nightmares of sharing a prison cell with the likes of Al Capone because I put a deduction in the wrong box. I've saved all my returns, worksheets, bank statements, and receipts back through 1988—just in case. Anxiety, fear, dread, irritation—can you add to the list?

So, even though the clean lines make Helvetica one of the most readable typefaces on the planet, I would prefer not to dredge up the emotions and memories connected to the Helvetican IRS. Remember this the next time you are choosing a typeface for headings and subheadings in your publications.

The Right Type for the Job

Type Is Visual

Words are images too.

What's wrong with this picture? Whether we are conscious of it or not, we are used to seeing words in certain shapes and orientations.[3]

As the Adobe Photoshop *User Guide*[4] states so eloquently:

"Typography gives visual form to language."

Type is emotional and situational. Just as you wouldn't laugh at a funeral or yell "Fire!" during a worship service (unless the church really *was* on fire), certain fonts are out of place in certain situations.

**"Sometimes it's not just what you say,
but how you say it."**

Kinko's certainly makes that point effectively in this advertisement featuring alternative business cards for a malpractice attorney.[5]

As type guru Daniel Will-Harris says, the two most important things to remember about typography are:

1. Type is on the page to serve the text. It should make the words easy to read and provide a suitable background. Type can be beautiful and decorative—but if it calls *undue* attention to itself or makes it difficult to read the text—then it becomes self-conscious and

distracting. Of course, some people will love this and tell you how brilliant you are—but they won't read the text.

2. There are no good and bad typefaces; there are *appropriate* and *inappropriate* typefaces. Think about your reader and the feeling you want to convey, then choose a typeface that fits.[6]

The Interview

George prepared for his job interview for days. Unfortunately, he wasn't really a good match for the nature of this particular company. In the dialog that follows, we're going to use typography—typefaces—to represent the personalities that George and the person interviewing him displayed:

George: Hey, how ya doin'?

Interviewer: I beg your pardon?

George: I hear ya pay big bucks here.

Interviewer: Indeed. Well, before we offer a signing bonus, perhaps you could answer a few questions. On the personal side, what sort of things do you most enjoy doing?

George: I love listenin' to Country Rap and the voices in my head.

Interviewer: How interesting. Thank you for your time.

George's friend Herb was a different kind of person—staid and traditional and well prepared for the "standard" interview. But Herb himself was challenged in quite a different way from George's interview. Here's how Herb's interview went:

INTERVIEWER: DUDE! WELCOME TO QUANTUM
FROG ENTERPRISES!

Herb: Quantum what?

INTERVIEWER: QUANTUM FROG. WE JUST ADDED
THE FROG PART OVER A 6-PACK
OF BUD LITE LAST NIGHT.

Herb: I don't drink.

INTERVIEWER: WELL, LA, DEE, DAH. CAN YOU AT
LEAST MAKE CROAKING NOISES?
WE HAVE OUR WEEKLY COMPETITION
COMING UP . . . .

Not surprisingly, neither George nor Herb got the jobs they were interviewing for—their personalities simply didn't match the respective personalities of the interviewers. Analogously, type styles have distinct personalities—and the typefaces you choose must be right for the situation and audience at hand.

Type Casting

PURPOSE	TYPEFACE
Legibility	Georgia
Dog walking ad	Good Dog Cool
Spelling bee	Abc Bulletin
Social invitation	Apple Chancery
Graphic artist ad	Futura
School dance poster	Party LET
Christmas newsletter	Calligraph
Business cards (formal)	Lydian MT
Business cards (informal)	Lucida Casual
Neighborhood barbeque	Wrangler
Chinese restaurant (sign)	Matura
Bible study: Old Testament	Old English

This table shows just a small sample of how appropriate typefaces can help convey the mood and meaning of particular communications. (Like a kid in a candy shop, I had to try out over 700 typefaces to come up with the best, most illustrative examples for this chapter. All in the name of serious research, of course.)

It's easy to get carried away with fonts. More is not always better. Imagine 500 words of text set in Good Dog Cool. While the paws are cute for the first few words, they would soon become as welcome as a real dog's muddy paws on the white living room rug.

Second Graders' Experiment

For one of their technology-enhanced projects, the students in Jane Gerlich's 2nd grade class at St. Joseph's School in Boynton Beach, Florida, have created calendars and illustrated them with their favorite recipes. (See Chapter 8 for the step-by-step directions for making "yummy" Jell-O.) Initially, the students just typed with the default typeface. As you might imagine, Times New Roman didn't exactly capture the whimsy of the project. So I suggested a little experiment: Show the students samples of four typefaces and ask them to decide which one they like the best.

Jane gave the experiment an interesting little twist. She let the students make their choice, and then she announced: "Good, then we'll use that Old English for our recipes!" At that point, the students protested vehemently: "You didn't tell us we were picking for the recipes. That changes everything!" Even in 2nd grade, they not only knew what they liked, but also which typefaces were appropriate for which kinds of documents.

Typefaces and Fonts

Technically speaking, even though the computer puts typefaces under the Font menu, a font is really a particular size and style of a typeface.

For example, examine the table on typefaces and fonts.

Typeface	Font
Georgia	This font is Georgia, 8 point, plain.
Times Roman	**This font is Times Roman, 10 point, bold.**
Helvetica	*This font is Helvetica, 12 point, italic.*

In popular usage, the word font is now widely used to describe the typeface family of characters (letters, numbers, punctuation, and symbols)—another way that computers have changed our lives.

Chock Full o' Fonts

What about mixing typefaces in a document? Remember how tempting it was to use every font in your collection for that first newsletter you produced on the computer?

Dear Customer,
If you have already
Paid the ransom,
please disregard
this notice.

Other than the ransom note, for most documents the rule of thumb is to use a maximum of two typefaces per document. Standard procedure is to use one *serif* and one *sans serif* that complement each other visually. The most common serif font is Times Roman. The most common sans serif font is Helvetica.

Document	Heads, subheads larger sized	Body text smaller sized
On the Web	Serif font (like Times)	Sans serif font (like Helvetica)
In print	Sans serif font (like Helvetica)	Serif font (like Times)

Why the difference in using serifs (the little flourishes or appendages on the letters) from print to Web? According to typeface designer Chuck Bigelow:

When printed, the serifs on typefaces are only a tiny percentage of the typeface's design. But on screen, in order to display the serifs using the limited number of available pixels, they take up a much bigger proportion of the information than they do on the printed page. Serifs should be small things—but on screen they become big—no longer visual cues but noise—distracting chunks of interference.[7]

Are you publishing on the Web? Try different typefaces and see which ones are the most readable. Consider using ones like Georgia (with serifs) or Verdana (sans serifs), which were designed specifically for the screen (and the Web).

Readability

What's Your Point?

Size of type is described in a typographic unit of measurement called *points*. There are approximately 72 points per inch. Typically, body text is printed at relatively small point sizes:

10 point Times • 11 point Times • 12 point Times

The Times Roman font was originally designed for the *London Times* in 1932. Because of its slightly condensed letters, it allowed for more words per page and rapidly became the most popular typeface for books and magazines.

Subheads are set in relatively larger point sizes:

14 point Helvetica Bold
18 point Helvetica Bold

Headlines range from 24 to 72 point type, or even larger for special, graphic effects.

Size Matters

Can you read this without your glasses?

Can you read this without your glasses?

Can you read this without your glasses?

Can you read this without your glasses?

Can you read this without your glasses?

Can you read this without your glasses?

Can you read this without your glasses?

The Eye Chart

One of the first things I suggest for anyone preparing documents of any kind (for print, projection, or Web pages) is to prepare an "eye chart." The text in the chart reproduced here ranged from 4 to 18 points. For printed and Web-based text, I rarely drop below 12-point text out of respect for readers with bifocals. For screens of projected text (think PowerPoint slide shows), the minimum font size is usually 18-point.

If you can't check out the presentation room ahead of time, a good rule of thumb is to stand 10 feet back from your computer screen. What you can read on that screen is approximately what your audience will be able to read when the image is enlarged by an LCD projector.

I have my eye chart on my laptop and always use it to do a last-minute check of my presentation in the actual room where I'll be presenting. I use almost no text in my slides, but I like to do the check in the name of field research.

12 point

18 point

24 point

36 point

48 point

Etched in Stone

Old serifs are actually a holdover from the Romans who engraved the embellished letters into stone. It wasn't until the early 19th century that type without serifs (*sans* means "without" in French) was introduced in Europe. Fonts without flourishes were initially considered so bold that they were called "grotesque," or "Gothic," labels that have stuck to this day. Franklin Gothic and Century Gothic are two commonly used sans serif typefaces, along with the omnipresent Arial and the bold Arial Black:

Arial Black is a very legible sans serif font. With its bold thickness, it is overkill for body text, but quite suitable for posters, signs, and headlines.

Script

Some of the most interesting typefaces for headlines and headings are the artistic, swooshing, swirling, playful, flourishing, script fonts.

Just the thought of using Mistral sends me into flights of imagination that include my moving to a loft apartment in Paris. I would be immensely talented, wildly eccentric, and a total Francophile—passionate about everything French, from the bread and fries to the cathedrals and Impressionists.

Think of ways you could have some fun with script type. Imagine the large nametags at your next board meeting set in a particular typeface from the table.

Typeface	Name
Apple Chancery	Steve Jobs
Bradley Hand ITC	Bill Bradley
Brush Script	Fuller Brush
Mona Lisa Solid ITC	Mona Lisa

Or, let students pick a typeface for their name, print it out on an 8.5" x 11" sheet, and then decorate the rest of the page to illustrate their personality (real or imagined) as suggested by the font.

Alternatively, ask students to work together in small groups to design an ad campaign for an event or a real or imagined product to be sold at a fundraiser. Use a script font for the headline.

CAPS Versus Lower Case

Allan Haley, author of *Type: Hot Designers Make Cool Fonts*, warns against using script fonts in all capital letters. "Set entirely in caps, script typefaces are unattractive and difficult—if not impossible—to read."[8]

THIS IS APPLE CHANCERY
IN ALL CAPITAL LETTERS.

This is Apple Chancery in capital &
small letters. Which is easier to read?

Whatever the typeface—not just script fonts—words are easier to read in lower case.

WHICH OF THESE TWO TEXT BLOCKS
IS EASIER TO READ? WHY DO
YOU THINK THAT'S THE CASE?

Which of these two text blocks
is easier to read? Why do you
think that's the case?

PLAY

play

The ascenders (see the letter *l*) and descenders (in the letters *p* and *y*) give us more visual clues and make the text easier to read.

Ups and Downs

Arial Rounded Bold	Mona Lisa Solid	Bordeax Roman Bold
long & short	long & short	long & short

As illustrated by the words "long & short" typeset in Arial (see table), Mona Lisa, and Bordeaux Roman, different typefaces have shorter or taller ascenders and descenders.

Leading

In the early days of the printing press, space was created between lines of text by inserting thin strips of lead hammered to a precise thickness. This practice gave us "leading" (pronounced "ledding"), the term used to this day for spacing between the lines of text. Leading is a critical element in effective use of typography and can make a huge difference in readability.

A common "leading" rule of thumb for readable printed documents is to take the letter size and add 20 percent. For example, with 10-point type, you would use 12-point leading.

But when you have typefaces with long ascenders and descenders or blocks of all-caps text, you need to have *more* leading because the letters take up more space. Typefaces with more space between the letters, like Georgia or Verdana, also look better with more leading between the lines.

Small Caps

What if you want to use CAPITAL LETTERS for emphasis within the body text? If you use regular uppercase letters, they are not as readable as lowercase letters. Moreover, according to current Internet protocol, using all capital letters means you intend to SHOUT at someone. The letters do have that effect—almost jumping off the page to scream at the reader.

A more subtle way to blend in capital letters is to use SMALL CAPS. Many typefaces include a small caps option. If you are using Word, under the Format menu, select Font, then in the Effects area, check the small caps box. The small caps have an elegant effect and match the "weight" of the lower case letters.

Upper and Lowercase Numbers

In spreadsheets and uppercase text, uppercase numbers look appropriate.

THE POPULATION TOTALED 6,540,325 MEN AND 5,324,618 WOMEN.

Those same numbers may appear too large in body text:

The population totaled 6,540,325 men and 5,324,618 women.

[*Note:* For the most part, we have become so accustomed to seeing "capital numbers" with lowercase text, that the average, non-graphic-artist consumer would not be jarred or offended—or probably even notice the discrepancy.]

For a more elegant, formal, typeset look, however, using lowercase numbers with ascenders and descenders can be quite striking. In a typeface like Skia or Georgia with "old style figures," the numbers can match the flow of the upper- and lowercase letters:

Skia 1234567890
Georgia 1234567890

Columbus sailed the ocean blue in 1492. (Palatino)

Columbus sailed the ocean blue in 1492. (Georgia)

Weight

Did you notice in the previous example that the Georgia typeface seems darker than the Palatino? This effect is from their different weights. The weight of a typeface may also be described in terms of "dark" or "light."

Weight is an extremely important issue when designing text for slide presentations or Web postings. Typefaces that are too dark can meld into inscrutable black blobs; typefaces that are too light can break up and appear to disintegrate. It's better to err on the side of *light* fonts, because they appear simpler and cleaner.

Compare the two columns of typefaces in the table and think about where you might use the different weights. Which feels more elegant? Which would be more striking as a headline? Would any of these typefaces be readable in long blocks of body text?

Britannica	ABC Bulletin
Cooper Black	*Carmel Script*
Nadienne	Footlight
Stone Sans	Humana Serif ITC
Latin Wide	Colonna MT

Tracking

Another consideration for on-screen fonts is tracking, that is, the space between characters. Chuck Bigelow, co-designer of the Lucida family of typefaces, warns:

> Collisions between characters become very annoying on screen—when two characters touch by even one pixel you get a lot of noise in the tangle of shapes.[9]

Typefaces that are spaced tight for print (Times, Helvetica Narrow, Britannica Bold, Tekton, Lucida Bright) would not work well as screen fonts. Lucida Fax, on the other hand, designed with extra space built in to avoid character collisions in faxes, would be ideal on screen.

As type-meister Daniel Will-Harris points out, both Georgia and Verdana typefaces are carefully spaced so the characters never touch—and that makes them especially readable as screen fonts.[10] They are included in Microsoft Word and are also available as free downloads.

Proximity and Alignment

How text is placed and aligned on the page[11] communicates relationships between the various elements. As we blithely type along, paragraph after long paragraph, we can miss a golden opportunity to help our readers along the path of consciousness and comprehension. We can use heads, subheads, spacing, and alignment to boost readability.

Notice the juxtaposition of subheads and body text, and also the text alignment in two examples, set side by side for contrast.

Which page (on the left or on the right) is more inviting? Which one do you think would be easier to read? The visual skimming technique works as follows:

Squint your eyes and look at the page. The headings should give you a preview of the text they introduce.

The page on the left not only sets the heading—"Music Sets the Tone"—far away from its paragraph, but also puts the same amount of space *above* the headline as *below* it. Because of all the space, the heading appears to be a separate element rather than directing us to the related paragraph that follows.

The page on the right puts more space (leading) before the heading to separate it visually from the previous paragraph.

In a similar fashion, the page on the right has indented and grouped the grading system specifics (0–10 points for Content, etc.) with the paragraph that mentions them. Space and alignment both serve as visual aids to comprehending the text.

Strategies for Successful Presentations
– Dr. Lynell Burmark
Content, Technique & Purpose

There are three elements to a successful presentation: the what, the how, and the why. It is easy for students to get carried away with the glitz of technology-based presentations and lose sight of the importance of the content, and, more subtly, of reaching their audience. One way to bring the point home is to design the grading system as multiplicative.

0-10 points for Content
0-10 points for Technique
0-10 points for Purpose/Impact

Music Sets the Tone

Anyone who has attended a Billy Graham Crusade, or even a church service, can tell you how an impactful "presentation" begins most effectively. The seasoned professional does not enter stage left and start telling the audience what to think, feel and do. Well, at least not directly . . . .

Strategies for Successful Presentations
– Dr. Lynell Burmark

Content, Technique & Purpose

There are three elements to a successful presentation: the what, the how, and the why. It is easy for students to get carried away with the glitz of technology-based presentations and lose sight of the importance of the content, and, more subtly, of reaching their audience. One way to bring the point home is to design the grading system as multiplicative.

0-10 points for Content
0-10 points for Technique
0-10 points for Purpose/Impact

Music Sets the Tone

Anyone who has attended a Billy Graham Crusade, or even a church service, can tell you how an impactful "presentation" begins most effectively. The seasoned professional does not enter stage left and start telling the audience what to think, feel and do. Well, at least not directly . . . .

Underlining, Undermining, Bold Defying

> If God had wanted man to use underlines,
> He wouldn't have created italics.
> —DANIEL WILL-HARRIS[12]

It's still most common to use *italics* for emphasis within text, and brief usage of it works well. But be careful not to use italics for long, extended blocks of text. It becomes tiring and boring to the eye and quickly defeats its own purpose. This applies to all text applications: print, Web, and electronic slide show presentations.[13]

Boldface type is perfect for headlines and headings because it makes them jump out to grab the reader's attention. For body text, however, boldface is generally too strong. Gentle emphasis is placed more elegantly by using italics.

You might say that italics *whisper* while bold **screams**. A little of either can get your point across. Too much of either becomes annoying.

On the Blink

As you read text across a page (or screen), your eyes can usually process twice the alphabet (52 characters) before you blink. Once you blink, you lose your place; if that happens often enough, you start yawning and soon find the effort too great to continue. For example, the next two examples show 66 characters versus 51; which is easier to read?

Once upon a time in the land of Fonts there lived some truly bizarre
characters.
(66 characters)

On the screen, the best way to limit the characters is to increase the font size:

Once upon a time in Fontland there lived a bizarre character.
(51 characters)

For the print medium, if you are using a standard 8.5" x 11" page, one way to avoid the blink reflex is to format your text in two columns. That way it's easy to keep under the 52 character limit.

If you have a lot of text and you don't want to lose your reader, sometimes it's a good idea to put your text into two columns, instead of having long lines of text (blink, yawn, blink, yawn) stretching endlessly, on and on, across the page.

Strange but true: The same amount of text takes less space if you put it into two columns. It also helps the eye to put a fine vertical line between the columns. The line works to keep the eye in the correct column, rather than trying to jump across.

Hanging Indents

When offering a list of items, many designers and type-setters "hang" the text from a bullet or number. The following list, from the Adobe Web site, explains some DOs and DON'Ts of good document design:

- Long lines of text are hard to read. Try multiple columns or, if you are stuck with a long line length, increase the leading slightly to make it easier for the eyes to move from line to line.

- Use indents and bullets to highlight important points. Use headings and subheadings to help your readers find the information they're interested in.

- Left justification can be easier to read and looks less formal than full justification. Pick the one that matches the tone of your document.[14]

Document Savvy

What do your documents reflect about you? Could your image use a little pizzazz? (see the illustrations that follow). Perhaps it's time to look at your content from a different perspective; it may be time to turn things inside out. Perhaps a little reverse psychology?

Reversed type
Avoid using italics or type with thin strokes.

What about using one letter as a graphic element?

Tips on Type

What's your personality type? Have you acquired a split personality, using different typefaces, depending on the situation? Or have you aligned forces with one font that announces you the way that Ed used to announce Johnny?

Or warping the text to match your sense (or my sense) of humor?

Can you top this one?

So, you think that's funny?

Maybe from YOUR point of view!

How Much Is That Logo in the Window?

Many companies have created memorable logos with little more than the initials of their names. Who could forget the clean, trustworthy-blue lines of IBM? What about the ubiquitous FedEx logo? Look closely at the negative (white) space between the E and the x and focus on the arrow until you feel the speed of delivery. If you squint hard enough you can almost see your package getting there overnight . . . .

Your Personality Type

Think about the documents that you hand to other people:

- Your school/district/company newsletter.
- Your end-of-the-year report to the Board.
- Your résumé and business cards.

Do they reflect your true personality? (Or at least the persona you want to project?) Could a different typeface help to communicate your message more clearly? More subliminally?

What about historical figures? Modern-day politicians? Could you (and your students) have fun rewriting their speeches, using different typefaces?

Think about designing *Thank You* notes where the typeface is an integral part of the message. Be conscious of the image your written words project. Above all, remember: They may forget your words; they won't forget your (type)face.

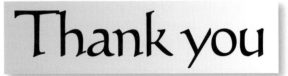

4 Color Power

Shoppers, for the next five minutes there's a blue-light special in aisle five.

This painting has a nice warm feeling about it, all that yellow and orange.

Hey, George, sorry to hear about your pink slip.

I guess you saw the red flags a while ago.

Good morning, class. Yes, it may feel like another blue Monday. But your future is as sunny as a little yellow happy face. That's not to say you're looking at the world through rose-colored glasses. I can see your true colors. There's a bright golden haze on the meadow, and we can color our world happy.

◗　◗　◗

In fact, we *do* color our world, all the time. Though not all colors have universal associations (as this chapter later reveals), every culture on the planet lives in a world whose colors have assumed powerful metaphorical significance. They have become common frames of experiential

reference. Can you picture that yellow "happy face" we just mentioned? Can you imagine it in, say, blue? It wouldn't be the same.

Stroop Test

To see how you and your students "read" color, let's begin with the Stroop Test. In the first chart, designed by J. Ridley Stroop, the words for common colors are displayed, with BLUE colored blue, GREEN colored green, and so forth. Most people can read this chart quickly, and without difficulty.

BLUE	GREEN	YELLOW
PINK	RED	TAN
GREY	**BLACK**	PURPLE

The second chart displays RED in yellow, GREY in green, and so forth. Whereas small children have no trouble with the second chart—they simply "read" the colors, not the words—most adults who are trying to read the words despite the colors will find the exercise frustrating.

BLUE	GREEN	YELLOW
PINK	RED	TAN
GREY	BLACK	PURPLE

To use the Stroop Effect as an experiment with your colleagues or students, you can download a ready-to-go lesson from the Web (http://faculty.washington.edu/chudler/words.html),[1] or create your own "Stroop Effect Tester Page" by photocopying this sample (or recreating it yourself on a word processor) and having students use markers, pens, colored pencils, or crayons to fill in the outlines of the words with colors that are different from what the word says. For example, color the word "BLUE" with red.

BLUE	GREEN	YELLOW
PINK	GREY	ORANGE
RED	BLACK	PURPLE
TAN	WHITE	BROWN

The point of the Stroop exercise, and all the other activities in this chapter, is to demonstrate that color evokes responses and contributes to meaning in powerful ways. Colors are the basic building blocks of visual literacy, the most immediate and powerful element of the images we see.

Color-Full Ads

Approximately 80 percent of a person's impression of a product is based on its color.[2] Imagine, for example, that you are in the dishwasher detergent aisle at the super-market and, as color guru Carlton Wagner proposes, that the soap boxes have no writing or brand names on them. Thus, you are forced to make your selection based on color only:

> Box A. Green, red, and white
> Box B. Blue, blue, and white
> Box C. Blue, white, and orange

Wagner predicts that the red and green box (A) will remind you of Christmas, not particularly appropriate for the job at hand. The blue and white box (B) will suggest cleanliness, but also gentleness, which would be good for fine lingerie, but not dirty dishes. When you see the *orange* on the third box (C), you will almost *feel* its grease-busting power. You will buy Box C, because it appears to meet your needs. Your autonomic response to the colors, rather than other aesthetics of the packaging, determines your selection.[3]

Color Me Interested

Traditionally, as educators, we think of color as the decorative element for our bulletin boards: orange for Halloween, Thanksgiving, and the autumn leaves; red and green for the holidays; red for Valentine's Day; pastels for Easter and spring; and so on. But color is much more than decoration. Color evokes a specific emotional response. We are biologically programmed to respond to the colors we see. When we see red, for example, our pituitary gland signals our adrenal medullas to secrete epinephrine. The epinephrine hits our blood stream, causing blood sugar to soar. Heartbeat, breathing rate, and blood pressure increase; and muscles tense. The pituitary gland doesn't care what shades you like or what colors are "in" this season. Its response is hormonal (not visual), genetically coded, and completely automatic.[4]

When should we use particular colors? How can we use them appropriately? What response can we anticipate specific colors will evoke in our students?

The Old B & W

When, for example, do we use black and white? At least until the early '80s when *USA Today* and other newspapers started splashing their pages with color headings and photos, we have traditionally thought of newspapers as a black-and-white medium. To this day, it still seems only appropriate to have solemn events and obituaries depicted in stark black and white. Historical photos—some as recent as Beatles posters from the '60s—also seem proper in their black-and-white (and grayscale) renditions.

It has been reported that recently a group of high school students complained when they saw the first photos from Mathew Brady's Civil War photographs collection. All 1,118 images were in black and white. Apparently it's difficult to take a historical perspective when you were born 25 years after color television replaced black and white.

The Selected Civil War Photographs Collection, restored as part of the American Memory Collection, and available online through the Library of Congress Web site,[5] includes emotionally powerful and realistic scenes of military personnel, preparations for battle, and battle aftereffects. The collection also includes portraits of both Confederate and Union officers and a selection of enlisted men. Here are Grant and Lee, from the days before color film.

Print materials from the 19th century—even the 20th century—relied largely on black and white because it was

less expensive to print than full color. Do you recall the art history tome that was required reading for college freshmen in the early '70s: Jansen's *History of Art*? Remember how it drained the life out of masterpieces like Claude Monet's *Coquelicots* (*Poppies, Near Argenteuil*)[6] by printing them in black and white?

Finally, Cheap Color

One of the joys of electronic media (slide show presentations, Web collections of art) is that color does not cost any extra. You can download the full-color version of Monet's paintings, plus hundreds of paintings from other world-class artists from the Web Museum (http://metalab.unc.edu/wm/paint/).

Even though it still costs more to print in color, marketing professionals understand the value of using color appropriately. Even adding one "highlight" color to an otherwise black and white document increases comprehension and recall. Xerox commissioned a study done by researchers at Loyola College[7] that documented how significantly decision-maker performance improves with highlight color (see chart).

Activity	Improved Up To
Time to sort documents	15%
Time to locate a target word within a document	74%
Accuracy of comprehension	77%

In a recent two-page print advertisement, Xerox Corporation touts the fact that color adds to the bottom line. Based on the Loyola research, Xerox claims that by using a highlight color, businesses communicate 55 percent better; invoices are paid 30 percent faster, and recall is 80 percent greater.

Why do you think so many restaurant menus are printed in color? Assign students to collect menus (with permission from the restaurant managers) and discuss the effect of certain colors. Why do retro diners use black-and-white patterns? Why do Italian restaurants often use red or red-and-white checks? Is there a correlation between color and price?

Think Pink

Why, you might ask students, are fast-food and coffee-shop restaurant menus printed in color? Why do chains like Denny's use hot pink on the pages where they list their temptingly luscious desserts? What image (and Pavlovian response) is evoked when customers see a hot pink cardboard box? (See photo.) How many cookies, cakes, and donuts did it take to "train" us to salivate at the sight of such a box?

What about football locker rooms painted in a softer shade of pink? Here's what researcher Morton Walker had to suggest:

Hayden Frye, the coach of the University of Iowa Hawkeyes football team, hasn't lost a home game in many years of coaching at that college. Part of his success he attributes to the colors of the home team and visiting team locker rooms. The Hawkeyes' locker room is painted blue. The visiting team's locker room is decorated in pink. The blue color gives the Iowa players a feeling of strength and aggression. Pink, on the other hand, has a weakening effect on physical strength and inhibits the release of hormones that contribute to aggressive behavior.[8]

And the gallons of Benjamin Moore's pink #1328? This dusty watermelon pink with a slight salmon cast to it (also known as "drunk tank pink") suppresses violent and aggressive behavior among prisoners, according to Alexander Schauss, director of the American Institute for Biosocial Research in Tacoma, Washington:

> Even if a person tries to be angry or aggressive in the presence of pink, he can't. The heart muscles can't race fast enough. It's a tranquilizing color that saps your energy.[9]

By contrast, yellow should be avoided in such contexts because it is highly stimulating. Theo Gimbel, who established the Hygeia Studios and College of Color Therapy in Britain, has suggested a possible relationship between violent street crime and sodium yellow street lighting.[10]

Color in the Classroom

What about classrooms? Could a coat of paint improve test scores? Henner Ertel, director of the Institute for Rational Psychology in Munich, conducted a three-year study to judge the effect of environmental color on learning capacity. The study found that the best colors for classrooms were light blue, yellow, yellow-green, and orange. The study found that by using those colors, teachers could raise students' IQs as much as 12 points. On the other hand, using white, black, and brown caused a drop in IQ.[11] Although the effect of color on IQ is only temporary, it might still be worth painting classrooms light blue in time for the next round of standardized testing.

In an environmental study with color and light, conducted by visual-arts professor Harry Wohlfarth and Catherine Sam of the University of Alberta, the color environment of 14 severely disabled and behaviorally disordered 8- to 11-year-olds was altered. It involved substituting yellow and blue for orange, white, beige, and brown and replacing fluorescent lights with full-spectrum ones. After a change in color and lighting environment, the children's aggressive behavior diminished and their blood pressure dropped. Interestingly, the same effect was found in both blind and sighted children in Wohlfarth and Sam's study. This suggests that color energies affect people in ways that transcend seeing. One hypothesis is that neurotransmitters in the eye transmit information about light to the brain even in the absence of sight, and that this information releases a hormone in the hypothalamus that has numerous effects on our moods, mental clarity, and energy level.[12]

Probably a few more studies should be done before we paint all our high schools pink to reduce violence and our middle schools light blue in hopes of raising students' IQs. But we certainly can take advantage of using specific colors to create specific moods for learning. For example, we typically associate sepia toning with old family photos, like the one here of my mother's family in 1923, when my mother (in the sailor suit) was only 7 years old (see p. 36).

The warm tint or light brown tone found in these old photographs was originally the accidental result of poor photo fixing, but once photographers decided they liked the effect, they started to duplicate it on purpose by using chemicals to bleach the blacks out of the prints.[13]

Today, in the electronic darkroom called Photoshop, we can add sepia tones to photos without resorting to caustic chemicals. Where students have access to scanners, computers, and Photoshop software, ask them to bring in old family photos and experiment with the sepia toning. They can also use Photoshop to edit the photos to heighten contrast, "repair" scratches, and otherwise improve the quality of the image. Using high-quality paper and color printers, the electronically enhanced "photos" can be used to produce custom calendars, portraits for framing, and other gifts for parents and other family members.

Just as the sepia tone can carry our collective memories back, so other colors can create highly emotional moods.

Experimenting with Color

To experience with students that different colors create different moods (and to elicit from the students which colors have which meanings for them), try the following activities inspired by the "Study Art" and "Create Art" pages of the Sanford ArtEdventures Web site (http://www.sanford-artedventures.com).

Mood Activities

1. Start by showing a series of paintings[14] that use color to depict different moods and emotions (see pictures by Caillebotte, van Gogh, Monet, and Rembrandt).

2. Next, have every student take a sheet of drawing paper and fold it into four sections.

3. Instruct students to think of four different moods or emotions and write them lightly on the back side of the paper. For example, see the "mood" chart.

4. Then ask students to draw a picture that expresses each mood on the corresponding section on the other side of the paper. Use colors, shapes and lines to show the mood. The drawings can be realistic, abstract, or somewhere in between.

5. Once all students have completed their four mini-drawings, have the students form groups of three, and ask each group to number off: Student 1, Student 2, and Student 3. Student 1 should show her drawings to Students 2 and 3 and ask them to guess which emotions the drawings illustrate. (Rotate through the triads of students so that all students have a chance to show their drawings.)

Alternative Activities:

6. Fold the paper into four sections and write the four seasons in random order. Turn over the paper, then draw and color an image to depict each season. As the other students "guess" which season, they describe what "clues" helped them identify it.

7. Ask each student to draw and color one picture conveying emotion/mood and post those pictures around the room. Brainstorm a list of appropriate vocabulary words. Then invite the students to use those words to describe how the other students' pictures make them feel. Have the students print the words on 3"x 5" cards and tack the cards up next to corresponding pictures. Ask the artists to review those words and then describe to the class what they were trying to express.

8. In a situation where students have access to computers and the Internet, ask them to download paintings from the Web Museum (and other electronic collections) to make slide shows. They should present the slide shows to the entire class and elicit from classmates what moods/emotions are expressed by the colors and images the artist selected.

9. Another interesting computer-based project might be for groups of students to create presentations on particular restaurants, starting with scanning the menus and then continuing with photographic images of various dishes, the table settings, the room (ambiance), the waiters (uniforms), the furniture, walls, carpets, the entry, and ending with the outside of the restaurant. A major focus would be on the colors used and what kind of emotions/moods those colors created.

A complementary part of the assignment would be to come up with a list of 10 words that describe each establishment and that are represented consistently in every aspect of the business (every slide that's shown). It would be fun to invite the restaurateurs for the presentations and see if the words and images matched their intent for their establishment.

Warm or Cool?

Another way to create an instant mood, through intrinsic physiological and emotional response, is by focusing on warm and cool colors. Hues in the red/orange/yellow area of the color wheel are called "warm," while those in the green/blue/purple range are referred to as "cool." The warm colors tend to be active and exciting. The cool colors tend to be passive and calming.[15]

WARM   COOL

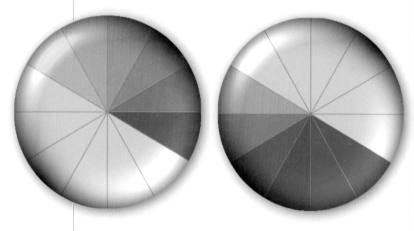

Again, paintings downloaded from the Web Museum[16] can provide examples of each (see pictures by Cézanne and van Gogh).

A wonderful resource for this topic would be the Cool and Warm Colors lesson from Arts Attack—the teacher friendly, video-based, Grades 1–6 art curriculum. Author-publisher Marcia Osterink leads groups of children in hands-on art lessons. In this lesson, the students view cool and warm paintings and then select art paper (from the blue/purple or yellow/orange stack) and paint a landscape depicting warm or cool scenes.[17]

Any number of variations could be done on this theme, from something as simple as having children fold a paper in half and draw a self-portrait in warm colors for their summer vacation and cool colors for their winter vacation.

In schools where the students do not wear uniforms, they could all come dressed one day in cool or warm colors, or in teams representing cool and warm.

Colors in Nature—And Culture

As with the warm and cool colors, most people have many general and universal reactions to color. Often, connections between a color and the feeling it invokes come from associating that color with its occurrence in the natural world (see chart).[18]

Color	Meanings	Associated With
Red	Danger, heat	Blood, fire
Yellow	Warmth	Sun
Green	Life, youth	Young leaves
Blue	Cool	Water
Brown	Age, earth, soil	Drying vegetation
Paler colors	Distance	Atmospheric haze

Funeral White

Colors do not affect people in the same way throughout the world. In some languages, there are only three color words: black/dark, white/pale, and red. Though many cultures do not even distinguish between green and blue, others have a dozen or more terms for blue alone.[19] Different societies often attach different meanings to colors.[20] A chart for yellow, white, and red shows some of the more well-known variations (see illustration).

Color	Cultural Meanings
White	Purity and virtue in Western, European cultures. Represents death and mourning in Japanese, Chinese, and Korean cultures.
Red	Danger in Western, European and Japanese cultures. Represents joy and festive occasions for the Chinese. In Vietnam, wedding dresses are often red.
Yellow	Cowardice in Western culture. Once reserved for the emperor in China.

Obviously, color/culture discrepancies (e.g., wearing black vs. white to funerals) are of serious concern to creators of Internet advertising. Because Web sites can be viewed by anyone in the world with Internet access, to avoid miscommunication dot.coms and other companies must reassess color strategies for advertising. Also, in classrooms where students have immigrated from a myriad of cultures, teachers need to be sensitive to possible adverse reactions to colors (like white) that have positive connotations in American culture. Having students draw images of what the colors evoke for them can help reveal these differences in the classroom.

Particularly emotive colors in Western European and American culture would include blue, green, and yellow. Careful use of those colors, as well as discussion of their significance with students, would be useful in a discussion of visual literacy. An effective class project might be to create a color concordance of meanings in world cultures.

Green Brides

In the portrait on the left, *Giovanni Arnolfini and His Bride*,[21] painted by Jan Van Eyck in 1434, the bride wears green as a symbol of her fertility. She is slouching in imitation of pregnancy, further indicating her willingness to bear children.

Similarly, in 1634, Rembrandt's painting of his wife *Saskia as Flora*[22] (on the right) depicts a voluptuous young woman in green, with her hand on her stomach and a posture and gesture indicating Rembrandt's invocation of a fruitful future for himself and his young bride.

On the "Color Matters" Web site of J. L. Morton, we learn that green, universally accepted as symbolic for nature and freshness, is also the most restful color for the human eye. It has great healing power.[23] And Morton Walker reports that—when London's *black* Blackfriar Bridge was painted *green*—suicide leaps from that bridge decreased by almost 34 percent.[24]

The Blue Madonna

The ultramarine blue pigment was originally made from ground-up lapis lazuli, a very expensive stone. Therefore, it was reserved for the most important person in a painting, such as the Virgin Mary. Examples of these paintings[25] include pictures by 15th century artists Sandro Botticelli and Fra Filippo Lippi (see illustrations).

Other expensive colors were vermilion red (made from sulphur and mercury) and gold. They were used for holy figures like saints, angels, and Christ, or for portraits of wealthy patrons.[26]

Practical Colors

Blue, Not Green, for Banks

One might think that, because money is green, the best color for bank literature would be green. But, as Carlton Wagner explains, "The bank doesn't do well when it is seen to be simply a money making organization. The bank does best when it occupies a position of respect, responsibility and knowledge in the customer's mind."[27]

So what is the best color to create that image? Wagner continues: "Since dark blue was first used as the color for the Virgin Mary in A.D. 431, western cultures have learned to associate this color with responsibility, a prime quality when you are depositing your money for some institution to manage." Look at your next bank statement. The color was no accident.

Blue Lights for Therapy and Growth

Helen Graham, a lecturer in psychology at Keele University in England and a specialist in color research, has posted this excerpt on color healing from her book, *Discover Color Therapy*:

> Research on plants and animals conducted by photobiologist Dr. John Ott demonstrated the effects of color on growth and development. Plants grown under red glass were found to shoot up four times quicker than those grown in ordinary sunlight. However, although red light initially overstimulated plants, their growth was subsequently stunted, whereas blue light produced slower growth initially but taller, thicker plants later.

> Rodents kept under blue plastic grew normally, but when kept under red or pink plastic their appetite and growth rate increased. If kept under blue light, the animals grew denser coats.

> During the 1950s, studies suggested that neonatal jaundice, a potentially fatal condition found in two-thirds of premature babies, could be treated by exposure to blue light. This same blue light has been shown effective in the treatment of rheumatoid

arthritis, healing injured tissue and preventing scar tissue, and in the treatment of cancers and nonmalignant tumors, as well as skin and lung conditions.

> In 1990, scientists reported to the annual conference of the American Association for the Advancement of Science on the successful use of blue light in the treatment of a wide variety of psychological problems, including addictions, eating disorders, and depression.[28]

Blue Lights for Dieting

Of all the colors in the spectrum, blue is the best appetite suppressant. Weight-loss plans suggest putting food on a blue plate. Even better, put a blue light in the refrigerator and over your dining room table to make all the food look unappetizing. Another dieting tip: dye your food blue.

With his tongue firmly planted in his cheek, international food consultant Gary Blumenthal suggests the following spaghetti recipe: Add blue food coloring to the boiling water before tossing in the spaghetti noodles. Then add few drops of blue food coloring to the spaghetti sauce. Serve garnished with blue M&Ms.

Why is blue so unappetizing? Blue food rarely occurs in nature. There are no leafy blue vegetables, and no blue meats. Other than blueberries and a few bluish-purple potatoes, basically blue doesn't exist as a natural food color. Consequently, we don't have an automatic appetite ignition at the sight of blue.[29]

Blue for Presentation Slides

Although we don't relish eating blue spaghetti, more Americans give blue as their favorite than any other color. It's restful and calming and evokes images of pleasant natural elements such as water and sky. In most cases, for most presentation topics, it is the best choice as a background color for your slides. The blue should be true blue (18 percent cyan, 11 percent magenta) or darker, such as blueprint blue (100 percent cyan, 77 percent magenta)—with no trace of yellow.

Yellow for Text, Highlighting

Remember the yellow marking pens we all used in high school and college to highlight the information we were trying to memorize for the test? There was a reason for that practice. Of all 16.7 million colors the human eye can see, it will go to yellow first. As Wagner states,

> The eye has an order in which it sees colors. Yellow, or colors with yellow dominating, such as lime green, are seen before others. When it comes to quick vision, there is no color seen faster than yellow.[30]

Red Attention-Getters

Red marking pens (the preferred weapon of English teachers for decades) also have a logic behind their use. Again, according to Wagner:

> Particularly yellow-based reds (tomato) are great attention-getters. They have the power to get noticed, quickly. There was an early belief that red (rather than yellow) was really the fastest color seen, and this early myth was the basis for red being used for fire engines and other emergency equipment. In general, bright colors, such as fire-engine red, are seen before dull colors, such as plum. Warm colors like reds are seen before blue or green. Red used in combination with yellow will get even more attention than either color

alone. The browns and grays are among the last colors to be focused on.[31]

In creating materials, think of what you want people to see first; what should have the dominant color. A yellow starburst can draw the eye to that portion of the communication. A phone number in red can encourage the customer to call and place an order. For other "information that will be looked at when necessary but is not critical to focusing response to your business, a secondary color like black is probably your best choice."[32]

Teaching Students Color Strategies

Our students need to be aware of color strategies, both as they consume information (advertisements, sales literature) and as they become producers of print, computer, and Web materials. These skills, students will learn all too quickly, are critical in New Economy positions.

For teaching students the fundamentals of color and design concepts in print materials, the classic resource is *Looking Good in Print*, by Roger C. Parker and Patrick Berry.[33] Especially useful are Chapter 12, which features common design mistakes with color, and Chapter 13, which offers makeovers of poorly designed publications.

For preparing images and media for the Web, the most instructive (and fun!) resource is *Deconstructing Web Graphics*, by Lynda Weinman.[34] As the subtitle "Web Design Case Studies and Tutorials" indicates, Weinman walks you through favorite Web sites and reveals the secrets behind their success.

The Internet has given millions of nonartists (and totally nonartistic people) the opportunity to display their idea of what looks good for all the world to see. For a while, many sites chose the strikingly nauseating color combination of black and red text on a yellow-green background—the kind of yellow-green that gave chartreuse a bad name. The red/green combination also creates a problem for many viewers with borderline color blindness. About 8 percent of men have some type of color deficiency in their vision, with the most common problem being an inability to distinguish red from green. Only 0.5 percent of women experience color deficiency.[35]

Classic Children's Books

Of course, no discussion of color would be complete without mentioning classic children's books on the topic. One of the best is *My Many Colored Days*, by Dr. Seuss, a delightful rhapsody on the propinquity between color and mood.[36]

This title is also featured on the Seussville Web site,[37] which includes activities for "rainy-colored days," including the following:

- Bake many-colored cookies
- Draw many-colored wax pictures
- Make many-colored gift wraps

Another complementary activity/resource is the *Notes Alive! My Many Colored Days* video, which adds music and animation to the Dr. Seuss book and illustrates how color and music can combine to create a mood. The delightful fusion of music appreciation (the Minnesota Orchestra Visual Entertainment at work), computer animation (see a boy and his dog frolic in various 3-D landscapes), and rhyming whimsy (the work of Theodor S. Geisel—alias Dr. Seuss—read by actress Holly Hunter) all show how colors reflect emotions and vice versa. The

60-minute video is composed of 3- to 5-minute segments focusing on different colors. Teachers may wish to show a particular "color" to create that atmosphere in the classroom: orange to energize after lunch, green to calm after recess, and so on.

There are dozens of picture books for preschool and primary grades that use color effectively. Here are three worth special mention:[38]

- *Hello, Red Fox*, by Eric Carle (1998). An intensely visual experience for readers of all ages, this is the story of Little Frog's mother identifying the true colors of his friends as they arrive for his birthday party. By staring at the brightly colored animals, then staring at a black dot on the facing page, Mama Frog is able to see the animals as they truly appear. (Carle has illustrated Goethe's color theory of complementary colors.)

- *Round Trip*, by Ann Jonas (1983). A simple, black-and-white picture book that takes its reader on a trip to the city. At the end, you flip the book over and the inverted pictures take you back home.

- *Mouse Paint*, by Ellen Stoll Walsh (1999). For the preschool set, three engaging white mice discover three jars of paint—red, blue, and yellow—and outwit cats and snakes as they introduce colors to young readers.

▶ ▶ ▶

Armed with multicolored posters and charts, multimedia computers, videos, and techno smarts, today's teachers have come a long way from blackboards and ditto masters. Using colorful instructional materials (like the flowers shown here) to accelerate learning and increase retention, teaching students to use color as a basic communication strategy in the materials and reports they create—educators are transforming their classes into colorful learning experiences, in every sense of the term.

5

Welcome to the Classroom!

YOU'RE GOING TO AN APPOINTMENT WITH A NEW DOCTOR. WHEN you reach his office, you see a sign over his door that reads, "Abandon hope all ye who enter here." Well, at least he knows his classical literature, you figure, trying to hope for the best. You swing the door open, and there on his reception counter is a little sign reading, "Expect the worst." You look around the walls of the waiting room. They're plastered with sayings like "You look awful!" and "We'd wish you a nice day but we're trying to cut back on our irony."

You're right—this *would* be absurd, and no medical professional would ever "decorate" an office in such a way. On the contrary, most offices are designed to look pleasant, reassuring, and inviting (see photo).

What about *your* office? Of course, your classroom looks nothing like the dark fantasy I described at the beginning of this chapter. But how appealing is it? What mood does it convey? Does it invite your students to a place of real learning, engagement, and hope?

As interior design expert William Spear explains, what we *see* in a place determines to a large degree how we *feel* in that place:

Patients just released from intensive care left the hospital sooner when the picture they saw each day in their room was a beautiful landscape or children playing. They remained hospitalized longer when staring at a vague picture of a tree or at impersonal medical equipment. They stayed the longest of all when given an abstract painting to look at daily.[1]

The strongest and most indelible impressions of a space come from its initial, visual impact. Spear continues:

First impressions account for more than fifty percent of the entire experience of place. We create impressions in the early stages of experiencing an environment, and they remain a nearly indelible part of it even as changes occur and we process new information.[2]

Creating the Visual Impression

The Classroom Door

Know the power of a first impression, and start welcoming the students from the moment they arrive at the door of the classroom. See how bilingual Spanish teacher Melissa Alatorre greets her 2nd graders at Scott Lane

Elementary School in Santa Clara, California. Lots of yellow brightens the warm welcome Melissa conveys (see photo).

Maybe you're thinking, "Sure, all that colored butcher paper makes sense at an elementary school, but I'm at a high school (or the district office)." The point is that wherever you are, your front door tells the visitors what to expect. Think about the doors to a corporate law office. (Consider yourself lucky if you have no experiential knowledge in this department.) Imagine 12-foot-high double doors, in exquisitely carved wood with solid brass doorknobs. You're thinking this lawyer is probably expensive; he must win a lot of cases. Bingo! The doors worked. Your checkbook is already primed when you walk through the doors.

Think about visiting a professor's office as a university student. Could that be intimidating? I recently visited the Drexel University offices of Saroj Parasuraman, widely published author and renowned researcher and authority on issues of work and family. The hallway in the School of Business was dim and foreboding. Professor Parasuraman's door was windowless and painted institutional gray. But on the door she had taped cartoons from *The New Yorker* magazine, plucking humor from the angst of the work force as it tries to balance job, family, and other important aspects of life. When you knock on her door, you already have a smile on your face—a portent of the wonderful encounter to come.

From the Ceiling to the Walls

When I taught English as a second language, my classroom was jump-started by what seemed at the time to be an inspiring workshop. The presenter suggested that teachers put key vocabulary words on the ceiling so students could look up and find whatever resources they needed. At that impressionable stage in my career, I was prone to accepting without "sifting," so I proceeded to make charts of more than 200 frequently used words in the English language. Bright yellow butcher paper served as the background for white "flash cards" of words. Related words were joined to indicate the connection (see "big-little" chart).

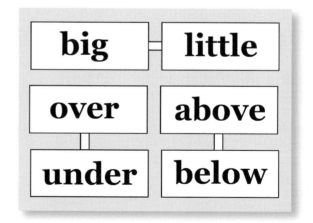

I carefully hand-colored all twenty 30" x 40" charts, then glued and laminated them. Then my father, whose undying patience has qualified him for sainthood, helped me affix all the charts to the ceiling. Of course, he had to ask rhetorically: "Please tell me you're not going to have the students lie on the floor and look up at these things."

Should I admit that an entire week went by with none of the students noticing the posters on the ceiling? Every morning a few more had fallen on the floor, as the masking tape and tacks gave way to gravity. I never did tell my father, but the second week I quietly moved all the posters to eye-level along the walls of the room. And that's the truth about how my famous *Wall Words* were invented.

A variation on the wall words might be *Mission Walls*. Does your school or workplace have a mission statement? A wonderful teacher from Vista High School (near San Diego, California), TeriAnn Mosher, sends me an inspirational quote every morning. I've started printing them out and taping them around my computer monitor, along the edge of my desk, and on the window ledge. Imagine those quotes on the LCD projector or an overhead transparency every morning as students come into class! You could save the 8" x 10" sheets and start a "trim," like molding, at the top of the wall where it meets the ceiling, working your way around the classroom. A template on the computer could create a top and bottom border and could continue from sheet to sheet to give a sense of continuity as the inspiration wound its way around the classroom. (Remember what I previously stated about problems with putting things on the ceiling? You may prefer to start a stripe, like wainscoting, around the classroom at eye-level. This would also avoid the necessity of having the custodian come to your classroom every morning with a ladder.)

Celebrations of Learning

Bulletin Boards

At the entrance to the St. Joseph's School Library in Boynton Beach, Florida, hangs a 6' x 10' collection of student art illustrating the "character-building theme of the month." On this page is a section of the drawings on Honesty-Truth.

St. Joseph's Librarian Jennifer Williams recognizes that, like the refrigerator at home, the walls of the classroom are prime real estate for displaying student accomplishments. She has created a winter bulletin board called "There's Snow Better Time to Read" (see photo, p. 48), with 4th graders posting oversized "snowflakes" reporting on a "cool book" they read and explaining why they would recommend it to other students.

Quilts

Several great ideas for quilts are proposed in Jean R. Feldman's *Wonderful Rooms Where Children Can Bloom!*[3] Although the focus is on K–2 classrooms, you can adapt

the ideas for other ages, as well. Quilts can depict any number of themes and use a variety of materials. As Feldman suggests: "Social skills will flourish as children work together to create a quilt for their classroom. Quilts also reflect community efforts and the beauty that evolves as individuals work together."[4]

For example, suppose you decide to make a quilt to commemorate a holiday or one of the four seasons. Feldman suggests fabric crayons. Students create images on paper, pressing hard to make their designs as colorful as possible. The teacher irons the images onto fabric squares, and then sews or tapes the squares together, adding a backing for stability.[5] (*Note:* The transfer reverses the images, so if students want to use *words*, they need to write them backwards. The easiest way I've found to do that is on the computer. You just type the words into

a program like Photoshop, which allows you to flip any image horizontally. Print out the image and then you can trace those backward letters. See the "ABC" illustration.)

As a fundraiser, 1st graders at St. Joseph's School collaborated with classroom teacher Judy Somers to create a quilt in the "South of the Border" theme. The quilt, entitled "The Storyteller," combines students' pen and ink drawings of important events in their lives, which they wanted to leave on record, and Mrs. Somers's image of the storyteller, prominent in several New Mexico Pueblo tribes (see photo). The border strips on the quilt are done in Seminole patchwork, a type of clothing ornamentation unique to the Native Americans living in the Florida Everglades. (*Note:* The parent who won the quilt in the auction donated it to the school library.)

The American Dream Quilt was created by an English-Social Studies class at Granada High School to celebrate the values they cherished as Americans (see photo, next page). Each of the 60 students had to create a 12" x 12" quilt panel (actually 13" x 13" to allow an extra inch for sewing the panels together. The students could use any materials they wanted, but their panel had to reflect their own personal American dream. The panels were created early in the year to "establish a baseline" dream. Symbols of money and religion were common. Family, friends, and career goals were also represented. Some students attached sentimental items. One girl included a scrap of childhood pajamas that had been made by her grandmother. Before putting the quilt together, each student gave a brief oral report on the meaning of his or her panel. Then the home economics class assembled the pieces and stitched on the backing and the trim. The finished quilt, about 6' x 10', hung first in the City Library and then prominently in the school's main office (see photo).

English teacher and co-creator of the project Jerome Burg reports that the most valuable part of the project was having the students "revisit" their original panel contents at the end of the school year. After nine months of "The American Dream" curriculum, many realized that

"higher level dreams like freedom and equality deserved some of the space they had given to their more mundane wants."

Informational Posters and Web Sites

Reminders about safety tips, directions for using equipment, and other important instructions can be made into posters that also create classroom atmosphere. Classroom teacher Mary Dibb from St. Leonard School in Muskego, Wisconsin, says her poster for demystifying computers is the most popular one she's ever created. To help students see what was really inside their machines, she took parts from retired, obsolete computers and posted them on a bulletin board with clear labels: floppy disk, CD-ROM, hard drive, circuit board, CPU, mouse, and keyboard. Mary displayed her poster above the computer workstation in her classroom. She suggests that the computer lab would be another natural place for such a visual. Asking students to create those posters is a good way to check understanding of procedures and also to see what the students feel are the important steps.

Nowadays, many time-honored posters are migrating to Web pages. Students promoting a dance or sports event or running for a student-body office are apt to send you to their Web site for information, color photos, animations, and even soundtracks.

But until we can all afford multiple flat panel display screens like the ones mounted throughout Bill Gates's home, there will still be a place for posters. And given the fact that Bill and Melinda Gates donated a new exhibit hall to the Seattle Art Museum, there is reason to believe that despite the Gates's Corbis online photo collection and the dozens of museums on the Web, there will still be a place for original paintings and sculptures.

Murals

Most major cities in the United States have murals in easily accessible public places. From *Childhood Is Without Prejudice* in Lake Park, Chicago, to *Louis Armstrong and His Heavenly All-Star Band* in the New Orleans International Airport, to the hundreds of mosaic, tile, and painted murals of Los Angeles County, California, artists have showcased cultural traditions, along with their personal view of history and societal issues.

If you live in a community with such murals, start by taking your students to visit some with particular local significance. To supplement that experience, have them find mural sites on the Web, or check out one of the excellent books[6] on the topic, such as

- *Street Gallery: Guide to Over 1000 Los Angeles Murals*, by Robin J. Dunitz
- *Painting the Towns: Murals of California*, by Robin J. Dunitz and James Prigoff

Ask your students to compare this timeless tradition from the cave walls of Lascaux to the spraycan-painted freeway ramps of our inner cities. Discuss how a mural would be different if it were to be painted collaboratively by several artists, rather than one person.

Look for ideas in the following mural projects conducted by inventive teachers and students. Then seek help from local artists or art teachers; select the medium, the surface, and the display location; and expect wonderful things to happen.

- Social studies teacher Michelle Beerbower reports using murals[7] in both Civics and Government classrooms to enhance students' understanding of the Bill of Rights. After introducing the document, she divides the class into 10 small groups. Each group picks a number, representing an Amendment to the Constitution they will depict on their mural. On a poster-sized sheet of paper, they paint their amendment using only pictures and symbols. Drawings, collages, paintings—any medium is allowed, but *no written words!* The groups have two to three days to complete their products. They present them to the rest of the class and then put them on display in the school hallways.

- Elementary school art teacher Kathy Black teaches students about the Ashcan school of art and then asks them to create murals in that style. She begins by showing how the early 20th century Ashcan artists of New York City painted their environment as it was, with all kinds of blemishes—laundry hanging out to dry, crumbling buildings, train tracks, and garbage cans.[8]

Black gives students two large sheets of paper, a pair of scissors, colored chalk, and a piece of paper towel or scrap paper. They cut one sheet of paper in a continuous, "toothed" line, from one side of the paper to the other, in the shape of a city skyline consisting of a variety of buildings of different heights. They use that cutout as a stencil on top of the background paper, and apply various colors and layers of chalk to simulate overlapped buildings. Then they add details of what they may find in the city, such as people, streetlights, vehicles, signs, stores, and so forth.

For students in suburban schools, you might want to adapt this activity to depict their community's tree-lined streets on garbage day (see photo).

This could lead to a discussion on recycling

and how other cultures dispose of garbage. Particularly if you have students from other countries where things are repaired rather than discarded, this could spark some lively discussion. (Ask students who grew up in other countries about Pampers, paper plates, and other such items that U.S. citizens dispose of every day.) Let the mural inspire an ecological discussion and see what evolves. The students may decide to create a second mural of an ideal city. (What would that look like? Would there be bed sheets blowing in the wind? Where would people put their trash?)

• Another interesting mural theme is lunchtime in the school cafeteria.[9] Groups of four to six students collaborate on murals depicting the cafeteria on a typical school day. Each group is given a five-foot-long sheet of butcher paper and whatever coloring/painting tools the teacher has available. (If using marking pens, make sure to cover the table first, because colors will "bleed" through.)

Remind students to draw their designs in pencil first, and explain that they all need to be on the same side of the table, to avoid upside-down art. And they have to arrive at a consensus on what to draw. If your school cafeteria has tables that fold up into the wall, you might suggest that the students create vertical murals that could be displayed from the undersides of those tables.

When all the groups have finished (specify a time limit, or this could go on for days), each group stands in front of the class and presents their mural and the stories behind it. Some students will make them funny. Be prepared for depictions of food fights.

Tabletop Projects

In his two-week intensive workshop on WorkLIFE Planning, *What Color Is Your Parachute?*[10] author Richard Bolles asks groups of six participants to design an "Ideal Island" (see illustration, p. 52). He provides poster-sized sheets of paper, Post-it notes, colored marking pens, glue, scissors, and a three-hour block of time. For this island, the groups were instructed to draw or put words or objects for everything they wanted to have in this ideal world, and nothing they would not want to have. The complexity of the islands varied, according to the ages and life experiences (and set-in-their-ways attitudes) of the participants. As a workshop attendee, I had the privilege of working in a group with people from three different countries. This diversity made for some lively discussions about our island.

Presenting the islands to the rest of the group (there were seven groups of six people in the class) was nothing short of awesome. Some touching moments, some

insights into human collaboration and compromise, and some bursts of ingenuity and hilarity that—well, you had to be there. . . .

This exercise can prove extremely engaging and enlightening in the classroom, as well. If you are doing the "Ideal Island" tabletop project with students, and your class is limited to 45 minutes to an hour per day, you would need to span the activity over several days. The islands could also become more visually complex if students were allowed to use materials from outside the classroom.

Third-grade teacher Donna Banting from St. Joseph's School is now using the "island" concept as a wrap-up for each of the major themes she teaches during the school year. Students build an Animal Island, a Pilgrim Colony, and an Imaginary Planet. Banting has the groups plan ahead and bring in as much material as they can fit into one grocery bag. On construction day, they have one hour to build. Banting says the hardest thing for her has been not to step in, to just observe how the students interact. In the photo that follows, Kristin is having a joyful moment as her group puts the finishing touches on their Pilgrim Village.

Students brought their content knowledge to the tasks in a way that made this activity a good demonstration of what they had learned. (How wonderful when an evaluation doesn't have to feel like a test!) What the students liked most was presenting to the rest of the class. They got so excited that Banting finally took a student's suggestion to put masking tape on the floor around each project to keep exuberant presenters from toppling over the displays. Students also came up with rules like: "Everyone gets a turn to speak. If you talk out of turn, you have to sit down."

Working in groups wasn't always smooth. As Nicki noted: "Everybody was so loud that I got a really bad headache, and I still have it!" Students were proud of their work and, by the third project, were enjoying the process, as well as the product. As Charlotte wrote: "Working together is our gift, and getting a wonderful imagined planet done beautifully was our prize."

In most classrooms, once the islands are presented, there is really no place to display or store them. In the *Parachute* class, we took multiple photographs of our island—and our fellow islanders—as keepsakes. In Donna

Banting's class, parent volunteers come in to videotape each presentation.

This type of exercise could be adapted to a variety of subjects, such as the ideal school, the ideal family, the ideal home, even the ideal life. Groups of teenage girls could design the ideal prom date or husband, while groups of boys assembled an ideal date or wife. Microworlds could be created with parameters: Think of simulation software like the *Oregon Trail*, where students have limited resources (and space in the wagon); and they have to decide what to take on the trip. Think of California where the power "browned out" as the rates went up. Imagine an island with no electrical power and no batteries. How would you survive? Design that island—and please feel free to send me and the governor of California any creative scenarios.

Tabletop projects can also serve to illustrate the work of an individual student, sometimes amplifying that student's experience beyond the classroom walls. A perfect example of an expressive demonstration of subject knowledge is shown in this display presented at the California State 4-H Club final competition by 11-year-old Coby Fournier, shown here.

Entitled "Wheel of *Fur*tune," the 3' x 4' poster shows Coby's research and the genetic traits Coby chose to breed into his hamsters. (His hamsters' healthy, sweet-dispositioned babies have become the favorites of several area pet stores.)

On another poster, Coby displayed his history of sharing with local schools, a letter from an appreciative pet store owner, and his award ribbons from earlier competitions. Encouraged by the interest in his work, he's taking his poster displays onto a much-anticipated Web site that will further showcase his research and accomplishments.

Visually Enhanced Instruction

Charts, Graphs, and Diagrams

Have you ever been in a budget planning meeting where the facilitator had an overhead transparency with a spreadsheet and expected you to follow along? Exactly how long did it take before your eyes rolled back into your head and your imagination helped you escape to someplace you'd rather be?

Some people actually do *see* the world as spreadsheets. Most of us hire those people to do our taxes. My accountant told me if he ran into me in the supermarket he would not remember my name, but my entire 1040 tax form would flash before him. Most of us don't carry around that kind of calculator in our heads. We still need some more concrete, visual representation of mathematical concepts. By reading and "writing" information in charts, graphs, and diagrams, we process and comprehend that information at another (perhaps more memorable) level.

The argument for the effect of charts and graphs is made dramatically as well as humorously in a Kinko's ad[11] where a wife has tacked a Dear John letter to the refrigerator (see chart).

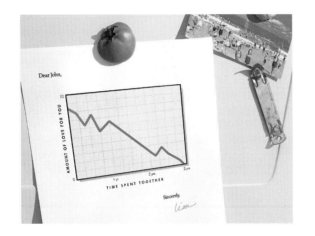

The first graph (showing the correlation between time spent and love felt) could serve as a launching point for discussion of cause and effect relationships. Encourage students to brainstorm about other actions that have consequences and assign them to turn in a graph at the end of four weeks that they can share with the rest of the class. (Wherever possible, I would ask the students to create these on the computer and project them using an LCD projector.) Middle school and high school students could plot things related to health issues and their appearance:

- Chocolate consumed and acne breakouts,
- Calories consumed daily and weight gain/loss, or
- Time spent on homework and grades received.

And what about the postscript in that Kinko's advertisement? Check out the chart, "Who to Blame."

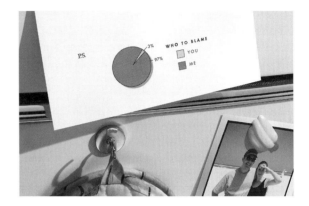

Graphing out feelings in this way could be quite therapeutic. I suspect if my late husband and I had been asked to design such a pie chart assigning blame for our messy house, we *both* would have drawn the same chart (assigning the blame to "YOU").

Who to Blame

Speaking of blame, consider how Peter Rootham, high school teacher from Ontario, Canada, teaches *Macbeth*.[12] He divides the class into groups and asks each group to decide on the percentage of blame for killing Duncan. He gives each group marking pens and chart paper, and has them defend their pie graph in an oral presentation to the class. In the graphing process, they come to understand the play much better.

Especially where there's a large discrepancy (as in the Kinko's "blame" pie chart), the charts can really drive home a point. Are you teaching United States History? How about the Civil War, where the North had 70 percent of all troops? You could ask students to graph out other factors that might account for the South's surprising success in the early years of the War despite this disadvantage in numbers.

Are you teaching Religious Studies? Have your students brainstorm multiple ways of visually depicting the battle between David and Goliath. This could be particularly encouraging for small or young children who feel they are not big enough to accomplish anything significant. A pie chart with four "slices"—Goliath, human strength, David, God's strength—could be an interesting way to illustrate the Biblical principle.

It's easy to get stuck in a "pizza and pie" mentality, and start thinking that all pie charts are round and flat. Keeping in mind that the image should support rather than distract from the point, let your students experiment with other forms of representation.

The Family Education Network offers a downloadable hamburger template[13] for students to illustrate how they spend their time in any given day. The relative sizes of the bun, lettuce, tomato slices, two patties, pickles and cheese can correspond with various events in the day. As an alternative to duplicating the template, offer students the opportunity to design their own sandwiches. Some may choose to represent some of their classes as baloney (hopefully, not yours), while others may feel more comfortable with a vegetarian platter.

Another creative "format" for charting is the flower. Before you start to snicker and say: "I just knew she was going to suggest that I cut flowers out of colored construction paper for my bulletin board," let me put the blame where it belongs: Richard Bolles' seminar on WorkLIFE Planning, held in Bend, Oregon, in August 1999. The original "Flower Exercise" is presented in detail in Bolles's *The What Color Is Your Parachute Workbook*,[14] on "How to Create a Picture of Your Ideal Job or Next Career." In the seminar, creating the flower was a two-week process, where each "petal" represented a different aspect of what makes up a person with a mission. Adults of all ages, professionals from around the world, became deeply involved with this exercise in self-discovery and produced some amazing flowers.

Although I initially resisted the idea of drawing a flower (sorry, Dick), I came to invest a lot of myself in wrestling with identifying my favorite skills, broadening and then prioritizing my fields of interest, being truthful about the kind of environment (office space and geographic location) I needed to flourish, and so on. I must confess I still have my flower taped to my refrigerator door as a visual reminder of what is important to me in my work and my life (see photo, p. 56).

In terms of the "Flower Garden" you could create in your classrooms, I would suggest starting at the beginning of the year with a photo of each child in the center of their flower. Then, as various projects in the year proceed, the students can add petals, stems, leaves, background, and whatever else they want to complete their self-portrait. It could be a study in self-discovery, à la

Richard Bolles, or it could be a celebration of their work and learnings. For young students, you might offer some flower patterns; for older students, you should just prescribe the size of the flowers.

Depending on what you choose to put onto the flowers, they can become quite personal. You could start by tacking up all the "centers" (the photos of each student), but then after two or three weeks take them down so students could "grow" their flowers privately throughout the school year. (Dick Bolles never had us share our flowers with the class. Some of us did share them with other class members with whom we had developed a special bond, but they were never hung up in the training room or used as part of reports to the rest of the class.)

At the end of the class or school year, each student gets to take his or her flower home. With their permission, you may want to photograph the flowers for your own memory book. These will be visual histories of personal and academic growth. There could be some real treasures. I would love to hear from you and to see some of the flowers the students produce (from those who are comfortable sharing).

Self-Portraits

To some degree, what Richard Bolles asked us to do with the flower exercise was to chart an *internal* self-portrait—a portrait of our innermost thoughts, values, and personality. It is also important to introduce students to the art of *external* portraits. You might start by displaying specific examples of realistic paintings and discussing with students what those portraits reveal about the subjects. If your computer has Internet access, you can download a treasure trove of portraiture examples. You can choose art from other times, cultures, and styles to contrast or to serve as examples for what you might later ask your students to create. Searching the online collection of The Metropolitan Museum of Art,[15] if you typed in the artist *Renoir* and the keyword *portrait*, you could easily find the painting shown here, "Madame Charpentier and Her Children."

Without identifying the painter or the subjects, ask your students these questions:

- When and where do they think these people lived?
- What clue might the "designer" gown give you as to Madame's status?
- What type of decor do you notice in the room?
- How are the children dressed?
- Why is there a dog in the painting?
- What other objects do you see in the room?
- Why do you think the artist included them?
- Does the room feel welcoming?
- What types of people do you think came to visit?
- Can you imagine some of the conversations that took place in this room?
- How do you feel about these people in the picture?
- Would you like to meet them or visit their home?

From the British portraits at the National Portrait Gallery, London,[16] you might select a portrait of Queen Victoria, as shown here. Without identifying who she is, ask the students:

- Do you think she's rich or poor?
- What type of work does she do?
- What's on her head and in her right hand?
- What colors are used in the painting? What does the gold represent?
- What is she sitting on?
- What is hanging over her head? Can you identify the fabric?
- What do you know about this woman from the painting?
- Do you think you'd enjoy her company?

I would explain that artists were often commissioned by wealthy people to paint their portraits. Can you tell when the artists were painting people they liked, as opposed to people with whom they felt no particular rapport? In which of the paintings reproduced here do you think the artist was painting people he cared for personally?

Before asking your students to create self-portraits, ask them to draw a picture of someone they know and would like to introduce to the class. How can they show their feelings about that person? Make sure they include lots of "clues" about what that person is like to make it easier for other people to get to know the person.

A stellar, in-depth lesson on portraiture from Sanford Corporation suggests that teachers demonstrate the process to their class:

> I want to make a portrait of my son. He is two years old and has brown hair and eyes. But I want people to know more about him than just how he looks. So I want to include some clues about what he likes in the portrait. He loves books, rockets, trains and cars. How can I show these ideas?[17]

You could adapt the Sanford example by using one of your own children—or a friend's child. Then, once the students are comfortable with drawing other people they know, you can encourage them to draw self-portraits. Alternatively, as you read the next example, you may decide to ask students to do one baseline self-portrait first so they can see their growth in later renditions.

A visually striking and exquisitely meaningful activity for self-portraits was introduced to me by bilingual kindergarten teacher Bev Erickson, from Scott Lane Elementary School in Santa Clara, California. Along one whole wall of her classroom, about six feet up from the floor, Bev displays a row of self-portraits drawn by her students. Her unique twist on this activity is that she asks students to draw a new portrait every month. At the bottom of each sheet, she has printed the month and year and left a space for the student's name. When October comes, the new drawing is pinned on top of the September one, and so on throughout the year (see illustation). The growth in drawing skills and the increase in self-awareness and self-esteem are documented by the progression of drawings. In many children, the improvement from September to May is striking:

Paramveer September 1999   Paramveer   May 2000

Self-portraits clearly chart emotional growth, as well as increased artistic skills. Art teacher Nancy Tompkins focuses on emotional issues in a lesson she uses with 5th graders.[18] After discussing what emotions are and which colors usually reflect which emotions, Tompkins asks each student to choose an emotion to illustrate. She then gives each student a mirror and a long sheet of paper. Using the mirror as a guide, they draw four faces across the paper, each face reflecting more and more of the emotion they have chosen. (Changes are especially noticeable around the eyes and mouth.) When these drawings are completed, students paint a large version of the last, most expressive face, using appropriate colors to enhance the emotion portrayed.

This activity could be extended by having groups of students write short skits where the interplay of emotions could be demonstrated by having each student recite her part, wearing the "emotion face" she has chosen.

Talk about early Greek theater, where masks were worn to convey emotional states. (How have television and movie close-ups changed this practice?) Discuss with students how they feel when they put on a certain face. Play the song: "Put On a Happy Face," and critique it in this context. Practice smiling when you don't feel like it.

For older students, talk about wearing make-up. How does that make you feel? Do girls send a different message with "black midnight" lipstick than with "natural rose"?

What about warrior paint for Native Americans or other tribal peoples? Disguises for actors? Religious and cultural practices (e.g., the red dot women from India often wear in the middle of their foreheads)? How about tattoos or body piercings on youth today? Could students (and teachers) learn something from explanations of what the ornamentation means to the wearer?

Do you see where this approach could be a rich entrée into any number of curricular areas? Visit the TeachNet Web site[19] for a comprehensive series of lesson suggestions. Like my teacher friend Bev Erickson, many teachers recommend having students do self-portraits during the first few weeks of school and then doing them again later in the year for comparison of both artistic skills and personal image.

Here are some other ideas on the TeachNet site:

- *Art.*
  Create portraits in a particular style, such as pointillism. (Imagine an entire wall of portraits made up of tiny dots. It would be very striking.)

- *Language Arts.*
  Write a short autobiography after drawing a self-portrait. For most students, more details about who they are will flow from the picture than if they wrote first and drew afterwards.

- *Science.*
  Take a nature walk and look for symmetry in plants and animals. In the classroom, ask students to look in a mirror and determine if both sides of their face are exactly the same.

- *Math.*
  Transfer students' images from photographs with a transparent overlay grid, to grid paper, copying square by square. Ask them how they would re-create the drawing to cover a 9' x 12' wall.

- *Social Studies.*
  This suggestion could make a great hall display. Ask the students to construct life-sized self-portraits as historical figures. They use their own faces, but they dress in "period" costumes.

Ambiance

In the classroom "ambiance" means more than just atmosphere. It suggests feeling good in a space, belonging to a community of encouragers, and thriving in an environment conducive to learning.

In this chapter, I've tried to give some examples of how visual elements can contribute to creating that kind of place. I've introduced you to Jean Feldman and her book *Wonderful Rooms Where Children Can Bloom!* I encourage you to check out more of her 500 innovative ideas and activities for the child-centered classroom:

> There is a powerful relationship between environment and behavior. If we want children to feel comfortable, confident, secure, and happy, then we must create beautiful schools where they can grow and develop to their fullest potential.[20]

Feldman talks about the aesthetics of a classroom and offers practical guidelines, on topics such as the following:

- Focus. Children's art should provide the color.

- Softness. Pillows, rugs, and window treatments can make the room look more like home than an institution.

- Order. Avoid clutter by grouping like items together and organizing the classroom so students can take materials out and put them away independently.

- Balance and harmony. Too many posters and objects in the room create visual overload and interfere with learning. Make the classroom interesting, but peaceful, rotating things to maintain students' interest.[21]

▶ ▶ ▶

I think the final word on constructive environments and exquisite use of visual elements must be from St. Joseph School's librarian and French teacher, Jennifer Williams, who wrote the following letter in response to my comments about the school:

February 21, 2001

Dear Lynell,

I feel very flattered that St. Joseph's Library gave you such a warm feeling.

Having spent my entire career in this field, I had experienced working in many different settings. When the architects met to plan this library, I explained the needs of Pre-Kindergarten through Grade 8. I felt that the more open the area, the better I could view our students. Many times there is more than one class, and still only one of me.

So many librarians have the unfortunate label of "bull dogs" who guard the books instead of sharing the love of literature. I try very hard to maintain an "open door" policy. According to my 8th graders, this helps them feel more relaxed and less stressed. I believe this is a helping profession, not one that should make life more difficult.

This environment becomes quite noisy with the little people, as we also sing and dance to some of our big books. Visiting parents don't seem to mind; they just comment on how bright and cheerful the library is.

It is truly a joy to come in every day. I hope this input helps for your book. My 6th grade has arrived, so I must end now.

Jennifer

From this modest note, you would have no idea of how magnificent the spaces are that Jennifer designed. Next time you're in Southern Florida, I would encourage you to visit the St. Joseph's library. It's the kind of place parents and teachers hope for—the kind of space all children deserve.

6 Presentations— Stand and Deliver

PEOPLE HAVE BEEN PRESENTING THINGS FOREVER. PREHISTORI-cally, there was the day Oog announced to the rest of the tribe:

> May I present fire? (Watch it, Urf, don't stick your fingers in there.) Notice, if you will, the lovely yellows, reds, and magentas. Now, you want to be sure to show fire against a plain background, preferably midnight blue, to best showcase its features."

Then there was the day Columbus was asked to present his case to the Spanish court for sailing three ships and their hapless crews over the edge of the world. "Ferdy, Izzy," he may have started, "As you can see by this bar chart, the burgeoning consumption of spicy food means we could make out like bandits if we found a shorter route to India. . . . "

We present all the time, in one way or another, informally or formally. No less in education than in sales or corporate boardrooms, presenting is a daily and indispensable tool. Most students love creating electronic presentations to show off what they have learned. Many teachers and administrators, on the other hand, dread having anything to do with electronic presentations:

It's that nightmare again—the one in which you're trapped in an electronic presentation from [heck]. The familiar darkness presses in, periodically pierced by a fiendish light. Bullet points, about 18 to a slide, careen in all directions. You cringe, but the slides keep coming, too fast to read, each with a new template you half-remember seeing a hundred times before. Somewhere in the shadows, a voice drones on. Strange stick-people shake hands and dance around a flow chart. Typefaces morph into Word Art.

But the worst is yet to come. As though you're watching a train wreck in slow motion, you look down at your hand—and *you* are holding the remote. (Fade to black.)[1]

A part of you wakes from the dream relieved. At least your years of sliding cardboard down transparencies, gagging on marking-pen fumes, and schlepping easels and chart pads are over. Besides, the presentation software was free, or at least it came bundled with your word processor.

Not everyone loves a slide show. In a notorious, on-the-record announcement, Sun Microsystems' president, Scott McNealy, proclaimed in 1997 that PowerPoint was *verboten* for his 25,000 employees. The ostensible reason was that employees were spending too much time preparing slides, presumably instead of developing content for their presentations or otherwise doing their jobs.

For the perfectionist, it's *easy* to spend *hours* picking just the right font, looking for (and editing) the right images, ordering and reordering slides, and experimenting with transitions and plug-in effects. Who hasn't squealed with delight the first time he constructed a *build* with text flying in from the left, the right, the top, the bottom, out of nowhere? What student hasn't put so much time into animating the title slide on his book report that he ran out of time to read the book?

Ironically, the *other* easy thing with PowerPoint is spending too *little* time, and turning out a "quick and dirty" presentation. A template here, some convenient clip art there (all included, thank you very much)—and in 20 minutes you produce a dozen predictable slides. Then, with the click of the mouse, you create your two-page handout by simply printing six "thumbnails" to a page. Of course, you also save time by not having to prepare separate speaker notes. You just put all the words on the slides so you can use them as a teleprompter. What could be easier? Or more boring?

Elements of a Successful Presentation

Text Versus Images

I never understood why people would come to a "presentation" of text that could just be printed out on a handout or e-mailed to them as a file attachment. Why not put something on the slides that complements the handout? Why not use each medium for what it does best? Print the textual data on the handout. Project full-color photographic images and video clips on the screen. I talked about this to my sister-in-law, a respected university professor and international speaker in her own right, explaining how I had started to replace the traditional bulleted text with full-screen photographic images on my slides.

At first she looked at me confused, but then a light bulb went on as she shook her head sadly and asked rhetorically: "Ah, you have no content?" It's all too easy to believe that the two are mutually exclusive.

Design School, Stanford Style

David Thornburg struck a better balance in the design course he taught at Stanford University. The students came into the course thinking it was going to be all about the way a presentation looked. He quickly clarified that they would be getting two grades:

1–10 points for technique, and
1–10 points for content.

Their final grade would be determined by *multiplying* those two grades. Even the non-math majors soon calculated that an exquisitely designed presentation replete with techno-flash (10 points) *times* a total absence of meaningful content (0 points) would not equal an *A* for the course.

In looking at presentations, I added and now teach a third criterion to Thornburg's approach: The perfect presentation must also show *purpose,* or impact.

A gorgeous presentation rich with content that makes no impact on the audience should receive a score of 10 *times* 10 *times* 0. If no one responds to the presenter's call to action, then nothing else really matters.

In sales, obviously, the successful presentation is the one that makes the customer jump up, whip out her American Express card, and enthuse: "I can't wait for a purchase order. I need your widget now!" (The academic equivalent is that student who comes up after class and says: "Because of you, Mademoiselle Burmark, I've decided to major in French.")

- Content (What)
- Technique (How)
- Impact (Why)

They are *all* critical factors.

Nuts, Bolts, and Classroom Applications

The next chapter (Chapter 7) drills down to the practical tips and strategies for working with design elements of presentations, such as bullets, text, color, charts, and templates. It also discusses projection equipment and high-tech classrooms. Chapter 8 then discusses digital images and electronic presentations in the content areas.

For the rest of this chapter, I'd like to share ideas on the approach to creating and delivering presentations. As a veteran in the field, I've been using LCD projection and making computer-based presentations for more than a decade. (Yes, I can remember when an LCD *panel* cost over $10,000.)

A New Approach to Presentations

You Just Have to Laugh

No matter what the presentation topic, humor can give us good insights, as well as much needed relief from stress. Humor abounds in our daily lives if we are just on the lookout for it (and have our cameras loaded at all times). On a recent cross-country trek, my colleagues David Thornburg and Lou Fournier decided they were going to take their guitars and "play all the big towns." From the road, they sent me the photo shown here (taken by Norma Thornburg). They claim the whole town turned out to hear them play. That's their story, and they're sticking to it.

Self-deprecating humor, as long as it doesn't insult someone else in the audience (e.g., I don't tell "vertically challenged" jokes any more), can be a great way to break the ice. When I was invited to keynote a recent confer-

ence of home economics teachers, my gourmet-chef neighbor asked: "Are you going to open with a slide of your oven? You know, the oven where you store your junk mail. . . ." She figured it was a toss up between that and the freezer full of TV dinners in my garage.

While I decided against showing my oven, I did end up projecting the inside of my refrigerator which, admittedly, I cleaned up for the photograph. For the segment of the speech on the use of color, I had installed a blue light in my fridge to illustrate the point that casting a blue hue on food—with the exception of blueberries and Diet Coke—makes it look totally unappetizing. The refrigerator was not as funny as my oven, but it was more germane to my presentation. (Watch for introductory pricing on the Blue-Lite diet system on my Web site.)

Imagine That

No one wants to read page after page of text on your presentation screens. Attack jargon with a vengeance.

Chop that passive voice. Slash those empty clichés. Imagine that each word is costing you $50 (see table).

Before (42 words)	Results from a survey show that two teachers out of ten have a working knowledge of how to operate the Hewlett Packard computer and inkjet printer. The same number of teachers has knowledge about available computer software for teaching written language skills.
After (16 words)	20% of teachers surveyed can • operate HP computers & printers. • use software to teach writing skills.

Granted, the "After" example doesn't say *everything* the "Before" example does, but remember that you, the presenter, will be there to fill in the important details and nuances. If the slides make you redundant, you might as well print them out and leave them on the back table on your way out.

At least 90 percent of my slides have *no words* on them at all. Instead they have full-screen photographic images. All the words we've become accustomed to copying furiously from the overhead transparency or Power-Point slide are in my handout or posted on my Web site. What's left are the really important parts of the presentation: the personal stories, the shared experience, the interaction, and all the emotion conveyed in the images that capture the essence of what I'm most passionate about communicating.

Remember, the handout should not be a black and white printout of the screen. The two are not inter-changeable. They play *complementary* roles—like the cowboy and the horse.

Images

So, where do you find all those full-screen photographic images I keep mentioning? The easiest way to get the images you need is to dial: 1-800-PICTURES (or log onto their Web site (http://www.pictures.com) and give them a list of the images you need. Within five minutes (Web download) or 24 hours (FedEx delivery) you'll have the pictures you need, in the size and resolution you speci-fied. Sounds too good to be true? O.K., so I made up the phone number part. As it turns out, not surprisingly, there really is a *pictures.com* Web site with links to gal-leries of great images (posters, drawings, paintings, and photographs). Unfortunately, it also has a section for pornographic material, so I wouldn't recommend sending students there. But there are thousands of "safe" Web sites offering photographic images. Usually the Web site displays low-resolution thumbnails. If you want larger, higher resolution images, you can purchase the rights to screen or print use of those images through a secure, online transaction. Museums and government-funded agencies are also excellent sources of images of every-thing from Egyptian mummies to Bob Hope's early days in vaudeville. Want access to 150 years of photos—over 500,000 images—from the Associated Press, including photos of today's news as it happens? Log onto the AP/AccuWeather Web site for a free trial (http://ap.accuweather.com).

I'm in the habit of checking the Astronomy Picture of the Day from the NASA Web site (http://antwrp.gsfc.nasa.gov/apod/). Each day there is a new image with a brief explanation written by a professional astronomer.

I'm absolutely fascinated by the photos, plus they help me keep my seemingly insurmountable problems in perspective.

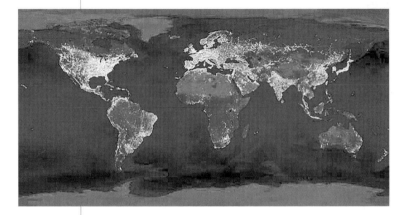

Reproduced here, this composite photo was posted by NASA on November 27, 2000. Called "Earth at Night," it's a graphic representation of the fact that civilizations spring up along shipping trade routes (along the coastlines, near ports and rivers). It also shows the stark contrast between technological haves and have-nots. Note the few lights appearing in tropical Africa. And notice the Korean peninsula—South Korea is almost all lit up, but North Korea is almost all in the dark.

Another site with "copyright-friendly images for education" is Pics4Learning (http://www.pics4learning.com). Long-time friends of education David Wagner and Melinda Kolk created this site as an image library for teachers and students. The Pics4Learning collection consists of thousands of images that have been donated by students, teachers, and amateur photographers. Image categories include animals, architecture, art, backgrounds

and textures, and so on. For example, the photo reproduced here, donated by Brian Page, captures the rugged peaks of Zion National Park in Utah.

The site lists citation information for each image[2] so students will get in the habit of giving attribution for material they use from the Internet.

But what if you need to make a presentation to the school board on the success of the school's literacy program? Unless you find a creative way to compare the rise in reading scores to the peaks of Mt. Zion, you probably won't have the time or the luck to find the exact images you need at Pics4Learning or anywhere else on the Web. Time to sign up for that photography class you've been meaning to take since high school. Probably time to buy a good digital camera. (See Chapter 7 for information about hardware and practical tips on composing and editing photographic images.) Photographs (and video) are absolutely essential to communicating your message. The downside is that creating a custom library of photographs can be extremely time-consuming. Let me put that in perspective.

Spaghetti or Pizza?

When I was growing up, my mother used to have elaborate dinner parties—typically 40 guests, and a menu that would take a week of careful planning to execute. For five days before, we'd clean every inch of the house, including places I was sure the guests didn't need to go. Three days before, Mom would start slow-cooking her famous spaghetti sauce from scratch. The day before, Mom would make the pineapple-carrot Jell-O salads and her to-die-for lemon meringue pies, and I would set the table with the good china, the linen napkins, more silverware than anyone needed, crystal goblets, bone china cups, and little personalized name cards hand-colored for each guest. The day of the party, the to-do list was grueling. (I'll spare you the details. Let's just say it involved punch bowls, shrimp cocktails, chickens, meatballs, way too many vegetables, and trays of yummy homemade garlic bread.) By the time the guests arrived, we were all so tired we just hoped they wouldn't stay very long.

What was the goal of the party? To create the perfect dinner served on the perfect china, or to enjoy real fellowship with good friends? In principle, the two were not mutually exclusive, but my mother's deep caring for family and guests couldn't always gracefully coexist with her demanding full-time job.

There is a risk of presentations becoming like those dinner parties. We can work so hard on creating the perfect slide show that we don't have enough energy left to present it. Connecting with the audience, inspiring them to stretch, change, and grow (or even just to buy our widget)—that is tough to do if we've been up all night working on our slides.

The flip side of this scenario can be equally risky. Imagine my mother deciding that if we kept the lights down and used candles, no one would notice that we hadn't vacuumed. If we closed the bedroom doors, we wouldn't have to hang up our clothes or make the beds. As for dinner, we could have used paper napkins and called the local Italian restaurant for take-out. Marie Callendar's could have provided pretty good lemon pies for dessert. It's possible that the guests at this party would have still had a good time. But I think my mother would have felt she hadn't given her best to her guests, and she would have been worrying all evening that someone would find some dust or accidentally discover a messy bedroom while looking for the powder room.

So what does food preparation have to do with presentations? As Editor Tad Simons writes in *Presentations* magazine:

> Thousands of presentations are delivered every day in this county, a good percentage of them slapped together at the last minute and delivered with about as much style and ceremony as a [take-out] pizza. Like the pizza, they may get the job done, but in a flavorless, unadventurous way that leaves a bad taste in your mouth: the taste of relentless mediocrity.
>
> More often than we would like to admit, professional presenters step up to the podium with just enough preparation to get by, hoping to get through the ordeal without embarrassing ourselves. Goals don't get much more modest than that.
>
> I know all the excuses—no time, money, energy, blah, blah, blah. . . . But we can all shoot for that next level of skill and mastery that distinguishes great presentations from the merely good or the barely adequate.[3]

Maybe because of the way I was brought up, I would agree with Simons that we shouldn't be serving take-out pizza. But how do we deal with lack of time and sleep?

I'm always looking for more creative ways to maintain quality. I've started doing more joint presentations with my Thornburg Center colleague, Lou Fournier. We are able to share the tasks of collecting and editing "the perfect images," collaborating on research, and assembling the presentations. It also helps to have a second viewpoint—especially on the impact of the images.

Your Slides or Mine?

The president of a large corporation is unlikely to prepare her own slide presentation. You don't pay people $5 million per year and ask them to spend hours working with Photoshop and PowerPoint. On the other hand, in many cases, when these industry leaders present their perfectly scripted slide shows, their presentations come across as "canned." The presenter could be showing a photograph of a proud 5-year-old and say:

> Here is a kindergartner being tested after nine months of using our integrated-learning, early literacy software program.

How does that compare to that child's kindergarten teacher saying:

> This is Chris. He came into my class last fall not speaking a word of English and not able to read or write his own name. The music in the Waterford Early Reading Program really broke through to this shy little boy! He's beaming with pride in this picture because he's just sung his favorite alphabet song, without a mistake, at the top of his lungs.

Which presentation makes you want to buy the Waterford software?

The Secret

Should I let you in on my little secret? You know how I keep saying PowerPoint is not a teleprompter? What I mean by that, of course, is that the *text* of your presentation should not be projected verbatim on your slides. But—here's the secret—the *images* on the screen are my *emotional* teleprompter. As the photograph appears, I am transported to the emotion I felt in that particular situation. Strong emotions are contagious. If only on a subliminal level, the audience will *feel* my emotion. They may not remember what I said, but they will remember how I made them feel.

I would not be as apt to feel such strong emotions if an assistant put together a presentation for me that I just saw for the first time 10 minutes before I had to deliver it. Using images to which we have no emotional connection is shortchanging our message and our audience. Images of situations and events and people who have transformed our lives (and, we believe, can transform the lives of members of our audience) are precious gifts, little pieces of our hearts, that we are privileged to share with people who come to our presentations.

The Delivery

Passion

When you teach a class or give a presentation, it has to be on a topic that ignites your interest. That may not be your initial reaction when you find out you have to make the presentation, but by the time you get in front of the class or the audience, you have to be passionately connected to that subject material. If you don't care, why should they? I certainly found it to be true with my students, kindergarten through graduate school: They don't care what I know until they know that I care. (I'd much rather hear them say: "Mademoiselle Burmark is kind of weird the way she goes on about French," than "I think she hates French as much as we do.") The key is that when you are preparing the lesson or the presentation, when you find something exciting, find a way to capture that excitement in an image. Then when that image comes on the screen, you'll be enthusiastic, and you'll pass that excitement on to the people who are fortunate enough to be there with you.

Attention Span and Biorhythms

According to the 3M Meeting Network, the average time a slide should be on the screen is 40 to 90 seconds, and the average attention time span of an audience is 18 minutes.[4] Television has probably programmed most of us to last half an hour, if we can get up and move around during the commercial breaks. (Actual programming time is 22 minutes during a "half hour" show.)

What does this mean for a 60-minute presentation? There needs to be a "commercial break" at least every 15 minutes. With television, the commercials are generally louder, punchier, and more visually compelling than the regular programming. And if, for whatever reason, you do not want to watch the commercial, you always have the choice of using that time to see what's in the refrigerator, move the clothes from the washer to the dryer, or do whatever you find more urgent than the commercial. I'm not advocating that we adhere strictly to that schedule, but we should recognize that television has accustomed us to that kind of rhythm.

Timing of Visuals and Retention

If your 60-minute slide show contains 60 slides, obviously you are not going to just set it on automatic to change slides every minute. You need to synchronize the slides with what you are saying. But do you click to show the slide first, narrate as the slide is coming on, or wait to start talking until the slide has been on the screen for a few seconds?

Consider the following research:

In a 1984 study conducted at the University of Colorado in Boulder, fourteen groups of college students were shown a 30-minute film that introduced an assembly kit, its pieces, their names and some of their uses. The film was shown in seven versions:

1. narration began *as* the slide appeared
2. slide presented 7 seconds *before* narration began
3. 14 seconds before
4. 21 seconds before
5. slide presented 7 seconds *after* narrative began
6. 14 seconds after
7. 21 seconds after

Students were tested on the film's contents immediately after the film was shown and again one week later. The first two groups scored significantly higher than the other groups in both tests. Groups 3 and 4 outperformed groups 5, 6, and 7 by about 30 percent.[5]

It appears that an audience will remember your presentation best if they are given the chance to look at each new slide for a few seconds before you begin speaking. People need to bring *their* own emotions and life experiences to the image before they are ready to hear what the image means to you. Let the image sink in first; then you can hang *your* message onto that visual hook.

Take a Stand

When you are making a presentation, where do you stand from the audience's perspective and why?

(a) to the left of the screen
(b) to the right of the screen or
(c) directly in front of the projector

Obviously (c) is the correct answer, because how else could you make shadow puppets?

But once you're through with the shadow puppets, the correct answer is (a). Why? Because in English we read from left to right. So, especially if there is text on the screen, you want the audience to anchor on you, then read across, then come back and anchor on you, read across, and so on. Particularly if you are talking while they are reading, it can be quite distracting to have you standing on the right.

One of the biggest advantages of the LCD projectors (vs. the old blackboards and the "smart" new electronic whiteboards) is that they allow the teachers, trainers, and other presenters to face the audience and to stand beside the image rather than in front of it. You want the audience to process the image and then discuss it with you. They can't be processing it if you are standing in front of it. And they have all that time to be bored (and seek other diversion) while they wait for you to turn around and step aside. Blackboards were a really bad idea from the beginning. Changing their color and making them electronic is like putting nail polish on pigs' hooves.

Here's Lookin' at You

Unless you keep the room completely dark, the audience spends more time looking at *you* than at any of those slides you spent hours preparing. You are your most important visual. What image are you presenting?

- Oblivious to fashion's dictates and societal norms?
- So incredibly gorgeous that the audience can't concentrate on your content?
- Sloppy, disorganized, unprepared, with tie or scarf hanging, buttons falling off your coat, and an unraveled hem hanging pathetically from the bottom of your garment?
- Professional, knowledgeable, credible in your dark blue suit?
- Caring, understanding, encouraging with your creamy yellow shirt or blouse?

How do you *want* the audience to perceive you? Presentations consultant Dawn Waldrop suggests that you don your normal presentation garb and stand in front of a full-length mirror. Then ask a good, honest friend (probably not your spouse) to tell you what he sees. For example, you might want to look highly professional, and your friend points out that your short-sleeved shirt or blouse is too casual. Or you may have on your standard navy blue business suit, and your friend reminds you the presentation is at a golf and tennis club where the audience will be in designer sportswear.

Once you match your basic attire to the desired effect, Waldrop suggests some specifics to consider:

Shoes should be the same color as or darker than the hemline of your pants or skirt. When your shoes are lighter than your hemline, people's eyes tend to linger on your feet.

Long sleeves project authority and a higher level of professionalism and garner respect. Short sleeves create a more casual appearance. Watch how people interact with you on days when you wear long sleeves, and then watch the difference when you wear short sleeves. The difference is subtle yet powerful.

Skirts should be mid-knee for women of short or medium height. Taller women should opt for a hemline that goes a couple of inches below the middle of the knee. *Women should be aware that the higher the stage is, the shorter your skirt will appear.*[6]

What about color? A major consideration is the wall or curtain that will be behind you. Just as you wouldn't put gray type on a gray background for your slides, you shouldn't wear a gray suit if you're going to be standing in front of a gray wall throughout your presentation. (One more reason to check the room out ahead of time.) Color also is extremely important because it guides the emotional response of the audience. It also can have a huge effect on how you feel and the energy you exude during the presentation. Why do you feel confident in certain outfits and less so in others? Do you think the audience can sense that?

What if you love chunky, clinking jewelry? Screaming ties? Exotic hair colors? Fortunately or unfortunately, dress code rule number one for a teacher, trainer, or any presenter with a serious message to convey is:

> # Thou shalt not distract.

By avoiding distracting attire and accessories, by wearing clothing that complements you and your professional stature, you have a better chance that the audience will leave remembering more about your message than about the quirky outfit you were wearing.

The Perfect Presentation

I hope you are as excited as I am about the potential for presentations. It's easy to be overwhelmed by all the technology, but I've found it to be less intimidating if I pace myself to try just one more little trick or tool with each new presentation. I don't expect to move from PowerPoint bullets on Friday afternoon to Technicolor, Star Trekkian Holodecks on Monday morning. I'm learning to see "the perfect presentation" as a work in progress—*less* like a book that gets fixed in print, *more* like a Web site that is always "under construction." It's as good as it can possibly be today, and it will be better tomorrow.

7 Dodging Bullets and Other Presentation Design Tips

LET'S FACE IT, IT'S ALL TOO EASY TO APPROACH PREPARING A presentation with a convenience store mindset: Get me in, give me some quick junk food, and get me out. Not surprisingly, the major tools available for preparing presentations thoughtfully accommodate this approach with astonishing thoroughness. This chapter takes you on a slow stroll through our metaphorical convenience store to see what's useful and what should be left in the Twinkies aisle.

Design Elements

Bullets

Mention electronic slide show presentations, and the first thing most people think of is bullets—those bold circles, squares, and little ornaments that work their way down the left-hand margin of most text-based presentations.

There's no question that *bullets* can be deadly. But to my mind, it's too much *text* that's deadly, and the bullets are the only things that are keeping the audience awake. In any case, we all use bullets at least occasionally as a

communicative-navigational pointing device, so it's worthwhile to think about how to use them well.

Jennifer Rotondo,[1] president of the Atlanta-based consulting and design firm Creative Minds, Inc., recommends keeping two points in mind when laying out textual lists of information:

1. Use numbers instead of bullets to capture and hold audience attention.
2. Avoid cutesy bullets (like smiley faces), which distract, and dashes, which look unfinished.

Rotondo relies on the Monotype Sorts typeface as a source of cleanly designed circles and bullets (see illustration).

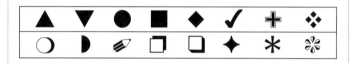

Have you ever wondered why we use bullets in the first place? (Besides the fact that they come free with our software. . .) When we look at a new slide, explains Jon Hanke, the senior editor of *Presentations* magazine, "Our eyes gravitate toward the graphical elements [geometric shapes, rows of bullets, and so forth] before we read the text."[2] As we design presentations, we can think of bullets and other visual elements as guideposts that make it quicker and easier for audiences to navigate our message.

Text

Once we get past the bullets, our next challenge is the text itself. How important is the *visual aspect* of that text?

Next time you go to a movie, or watch one on television, pay close attention to the titles that cross the screen. Observe how the designer has chosen specific shapes of letters to suggest a particular atmosphere even before the film starts. (Refer to Chapter 3 in this book for an in-depth discussion of fonts and typefaces.) Clearly the typeface must match the subject matter (see illustration).

Annual Budget Report

Heroes of the Old Testament

Games for Energizing Workshops

The next consideration for choosing text for a presentation is *room size*. In an intimate setting, you could try typefaces like Apple Garamond or Times New Roman. In a larger room, however, these elegant serif fonts would be hard for people in the back rows to decipher. Be especially careful not to fall prey to the drop shadow temptation. The shadows behind the letters only obscure the serifs and make the letters look blurred together. Sans serif fonts like Verdana or Arial are easier to read on the screen, particularly for smaller print such as chart labels. In boldface, these fonts also make strong titles, as the illustration shows.

Impact

Verdana

Arial Black

For presentations (and Web pages), Verdana is probably the most readable font (of the three) because even in

boldface type, the letters are spaced far enough apart to make it easy to distinguish each letter.

What about using *all capital letters* for the title of the presentation? Although capital letters traditionally connoted something important, lately they have become more of an annoyance. They are much harder to read and, on the Internet, all caps signify that you are shouting at someone. As Endicott puts it: "Instead of thinking, 'Hmm, this must be important,' your audience is likely to wonder whether you knew your caps-lock key was on."[3]

For presentation *font size*, bigger is better. A rough pretest is to look at your computer screen from 10 feet back, squint a little, and see if you can read the text. (How's that for scientific precision?) When we adhere to the "6 x 6" rule—no more than six words across and no more than six lines down—we are probably not going to use a font smaller than 24-point in any case.

Always *spell check* your presentation. When we look at text, our brains are good at jumping to conclusions. That is one reason it is so difficult to proof for spelling errors. We try to make sense of the letters, so we "see" what we think should be there.

The Exploratorium's Brain Explorer[4] includes an intriguing puzzle (see illustration), which asks you to read the words even though part of the letters are covered:

JUMPING TO CONCLUSIONS

Then you remove the black bar and look at the letters that are actually underneath.

IUMRING TQ GQNGIUSIQNS

We've all seen spelling errors that were hysterically funny, particularly because other people had made them. The best one I've seen lately was from a local college announcing a new program for educational leadership. One of the selling points of the program was that participants would be studying "in pears." (They will forgive me if I don't give you the name of the college.)

Computerized spelling checkers have been a godsend to students and teachers alike. I can't even begin to estimate the amount of red ink that has been saved by teachers who longer face the "creativity" that students like my brother used to display in their compositions. (Once, when I asked my brother why he spelled the same word three different ways in one paragraph, he replied without hesitation: "That way I have more chances of getting it right.")

Dan Quayle will probably never live down the "potatoe" spelling incident. Proofing is always a good idea—especially if you're going to be writing on a blackboard on national television or making any kind of public presentation. If possible, ask a friend or colleague—who did not work on the presentation—to double-check it for you. Then, in the presentation, always have a "prize" handy, so in case someone spots an error that you missed, you can pull out the prize and give it to the "brilliant person who spotted my 'intentional' mistake. Just wanted to see if you were paying attention."

In what *direction* do we read a page? Our eyes scan a slide (or a page) from the top left corner to the bottom right corner. Why, then, do we center titles? To make it *harder* for the eye to go back to the beginning of the first line/bullet point? But PowerPoint makes it so *easy* to center the titles!

On the next presentation you create, try lining the title up with the left-hand margin. Think of it as another gift to your audience.

Colors for Backgrounds and Text

Color is probably the most critical consideration in designing a presentation. (See Chapter 4 for an in-depth discussion of color.) Which colors should we use? Which ones for text? Which ones for backgrounds? And in what combinations? By far the most important criterion is legibility. Graphics and text need to contrast enough with the background to be easily read.

Backgrounds. Should you use dark text on a light background or light text on a dark background? Although black ink on white paper is the most readable color combination in print format, on the projected screen darker colors generally make better backgrounds. Light backgrounds can sometimes be glaring. (Remember how unpleasant it used to be to have the overhead projector on with no transparency, just the bright light on the white screen?)

Deep shades of blue and green are good for backgrounds because they are calming, and these cool colors tend to recede. The warm colors (yellow, orange, and red) are better for the foreground text and graphical elements. Think of the midnight sky with a gold-tinted moon and stars. You see the constellations more clearly because they seem to jump out from dark background. Think of a field of daffodils with the clear blue sky above (and in the distance). Of the 16.7 million colors the human eye can see (and most computers can project), the eye will go first to yellow. I have found yellow letters on a blue background to be the most compelling color combination. The contrast is excellent (so the legibility is not compromised), and the eye goes exactly where I want it to go.

Green is becoming an increasingly popular background color. *Presentations* magazine editor Jon Hanke suggests that this is because green stimulates interaction, making deep greens and teals particularly good colors for trainers, educators, and others using their presentations to generate discussions.[5]

I often intersperse black slides—or the fade-to-black "transition" between slides—to indicate when I have completed one thought or concept and am ready to move on to the next. (Notice that technique in movies, particularly when there is a change of scene.)

Text. Just as *background* colors set the emotional tone for your presentation, *foreground* colors determine how well the audience understands and remembers your message. Hanke states:

> It goes without saying that items are more noticeable when they're visibly different from surrounding items. Research has shown that the effective use of selective contrast—known as the von Restorff, or isolation, effect—makes audiences *remember* the outstanding item better as well. A 1982 Daemon College study concludes that highlighting or emphasizing meaningful text results in better retention—not just for the highlighted item, but for the *entire message*.[6]

What about red as a foreground color? Think about advertisements you've seen where most of the layout is black text on a white background, but the 800 number is in red. When you are ready to call, you have no problem finding the number!

As Hanke cites from *Purpose, Movement, Color*, by Tom and Rich Mucciolo, red is powerful and dangerous at the same time:

> While red implies fear, danger, STOP (signs), and financial disaster, it can also elicit the emotions of desire, passion and competitiveness.

> Research has shown that the color red can produce a physiological response in viewers by slightly increasing our pulse and breathing rates. Some studies suggest that red subliminally encourages us to engage in risk-taking behavior—one reason the lighting and decor in casinos often has red undertones.

> In presentations, red is one of the most powerful colors in your palette.[7]

Regarding red, it's worth noting that men and women prefer different shades. In fact, as early as kindergarten, little boys are leaning towards the warm end of the spectrum (rust, mahogany, brick, and crimson). Little girls are already drawn to the burgundy, maroon, and cranberry crayons in the Crayola box. Of course, every good car salesman shows the husband a fire-engine red Corvette and the wife a maroon Jaguar. It's what nature intended.

Another potential issue with red is that at least 15 to 25 percent of the population (mostly males) find it difficult to distinguish red from green. Even without the red/green color deficiency, the way our eyes work is that colors opposite each other on the color wheel (red/green, yellow/purple, and orange/blue) appear to move or vibrate if they are placed side by side. Clearly, when we create pie charts and bar graphs, we should not put red and green elements next to one another,[8] nor should we ask little boys to glue Christmas chains from strips of red and green construction paper!

The Art of the Chart

Besides rows of text and bullets, what else do Power-Point and its siblings Word and Excel leap to automate for us? Charts, graphs, and tables! It's another way to focus the audience's attention on your message, and another way to spend hours and hours on your presentation.

Take, for example, the astounding improvement in students' reading scores that the use of boldface can emphasize (see illustration).

May 1998	**46%**
May 1999	**76%**
May 2000	**98%**
May 2001	**100%**

The problem with this simple list, though presented in boldface, is that, at first glance, nothing tells the eyes whether to read down the columns or across the rows.

Compare that to the table that follows, using the concept of an accountant's "greenbar," or a checkbook register, where every other line is shaded to make it easier for the eye to travel horizontally across each row.

Date	Percent
May 1998	**46%**
May 1999	**76%**
May 2000	**98%**
May 2001	**100%**

Of course, this kind of information could also be displayed as a bar graph; further helping the audience *see* the improvement in reading scores (see illustration).

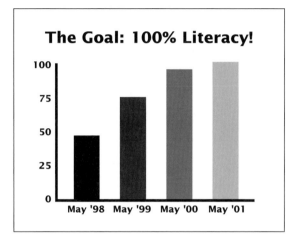

You may notice the subtle lightening of the gray bars (from 80 percent black to 60 percent, 40 percent, and then 20 percent). Why would I do that? Because the eye moves from dark to light, so that is one more subliminal way to force the viewer's eyes to move across the graph.

If the slide were in color, I would have a solid black background, with the bars changing from red on the left—reinforcing the danger of over 50 percent of the students reading below grade level—through orange and yellow orange to the bright yellow bar of triumph on the right. (Drum roll, please.)

In the spirit of good-is-never-enough for a live slide show, I would further dramatize the point of raising reading scores by resorting to *builds* and *transitions*—better known by their technical names: *bells* and *whistles* (see illustration).

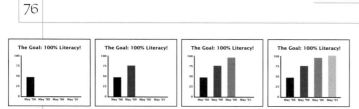

Instead of just presenting the fourth slide as a *fait accompli* (yawn), I would move through the four slides using a special effect called a "wipe up" (bottom to top) transition between slides. That way, each of the bars appears to "grow" as it comes on the screen. (Although the entire slide "wipes up," only the new bar appears to be moving because all the other items are actually painting over the exact same image from the previous slide.)

Why are these justifiable bells and whistles? Because the graphic and the transition work together to illustrate and reinforce the message:

More and more of our kids are learning to read!

Another option is to present the data in a line graph (often referred to as a "fever chart" because hospitals commonly use this type of chart to plot patients' temperatures) (see illustration).

The chart on the left shows the growth over four years; the one on the right just plots the starting point

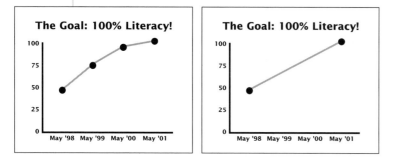

(dismal) and the current achievement (stellar). At the risk of being too cutesy, I might consider using a star (rather than a circle) for the final point.

By this time, you are probably wondering—hmmm, she's done a table, bar graph, and line graph; now how is she going to put this information into a pie chart?

Actually, I'm not going to use a pie chart here, because I don't think this "literacy achievement" information lends itself to that kind of representation. Other parts of the 100-percent literacy story, however, could well be diagrammed in a pie chart. For example, looking at the percentage of students who

- are enrolled in Spanish bilingual classrooms,
- receive Reading Recovery tutoring versus other interventions, and
- have English as a second language (diagram other languages spoken).

Each type of table or chart excels in presenting information in a particular way. As Nigel Holmes, master cartographer and former graphics director at *Time* magazine, explains: "The key is to focus on the purpose of the chart; then the visual solution will take care of itself."[9]

Holmes's sage advice is to keep it simple, as follows:

- **The best charts are two-dimensional.** You don't need a chart to jump off the page by using 3-D effects. I'd prefer for the chart to stay there and let me read it.

- **Set the chart against a solid background.** Use a white or pale background so the information is visible and legible. Brightly colored backgrounds, intended to enliven a dull chart, often obscure the data you're trying to relay because they draw the eye toward the background and away from the chart's information. An alternative to a light background is to set the whole chart against black, but if the type is too small . . . there's a danger that it won't be readable. Avoid photographic backgrounds; they interfere with legibility.

- **Start with black and white.** Add color only when you need to clarify something—for instance to differentiate between two lines in a fever chart. Think of color as information in itself, not as decoration to apply to the chart when you have finished. If you decide that you do need color to emphasize a point, red would be my first choice if the background were pale, because red contrasts most with black and white. On a black background, red tends to disappear; yellow stands out best—that's why so many road signs are black and yellow.

- **Use only one typeface in a variety of weights and sizes.** Ornate, decorative fonts have no place in charts. The best fonts for charts are simple, sans serifs—fonts without appendages at the tips of the main strokes—because they are easier to read in small sizes. Numbers also look best when set in a sans serif, because the lines of the font are so clean.[10]

A warning about so-called "special effects": Just because it's easy to use them doesn't mean they're really special. In particular, stay away from busy backgrounds that distract from your information. Avoid flowery typefaces, unless you're talking about flowers. And in most design classes, purposeless use of 3-D effects will get you a *D* grade.

Remember, there is no extra credit (in fact no credit at all) for gratuitous glitz. Any graphic elements and *all* whiz-bang pizzazz have to serve your point. Very often, less really is more. I'm emphasizing this so strongly because this point is probably the single most common—and disastrous—mistake made with presentations.

Templates

I would be remiss not to mention one more freebie that comes with most presentation software: predesigned templates, complete with color suggestions and graphical elements. "Yes, your presentations can look like those of thousands of other professionals," these all-too-convenient templates want you to believe. The risk is that your audience will fall asleep, comfortably assuming they've seen it all before.

You may still decide to use one (or more) of those prepackaged templates. If you do, please make sure to avoid the three deadly template sins, as follows.

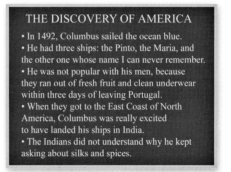

THE DISCOVERY OF AMERICA
- In 1492, Columbus sailed the ocean blue.
- He had three ships: the Pinto, the Maria, and the other one whose name I can never remember.
- He was not popular with his men, because they ran out of fresh fruit and clean underwear within three days of leaving Portugal.
- When they got to the East Coast of North America, Columbus was really excited to have landed his ships in India.
- The Indians did not understand why he kept asking about silks and spices.

Template 1 (The Discovery of America, above): Although this template offers good color contrast the original has a dark blue background with yellow title text and white body text), it would be more appropriate as a teleprompter screen than as a template for effective visual communication.

Template 2 (diagonal stripes, p. 78): I elected to show you this template before adding the text so you could savor the diagonal lines (in the original, deep

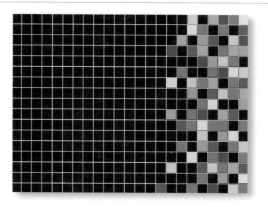

green) strobing against the background (in the original, chartreuse green).

Now imagine the recommended yellow-orange text on that vibrating greenish background. As the eyes struggle to read the fine print (imagine *serif* fonts, to heighten the visual confusion), they move diagonally down the page, from top left to lower right. Interesting collisions occur as the eyes bump up against the deep green lines going the opposite direction.

Somewhere in the middle of the page, the eyes shift from the screen to the briefcase, in search of that elusive bottle of Tylenol.

Template 3 (grids and blocks): This is my all-time favorite "professionally designed" *disastrous* template. A similar template, professionally designed, used to be shipped free with a previous version of one type of presentation software. (It's now available only as a collector's item.) I would love to have you see it in its full blazing color—jet-black background with white grid lines and wildly colored blocks sprinkled on the right edge of the screen. Even in this grayscale rendition, you get a glimmer of the challenges to the viewer.

The grid in this template puts you behind some kind of security fence. As text scrolls from left to right across the page, some graphic element (bullets, for example) *should* draw the eye back to the left. Alas, your poor, confused eyes keep getting pulled over to the fluorescent "dog kibble" on the right. Instead of helping with the communication, the template fights it.

So, what would I recommend? I see three options:

1. Go through the template collections (some are packaged free with your software; tons of additional ones are free on the Internet or available through mail order and computer stores) until you find one that has the right "look and feel."
2. Design your own templates. The background can be as simple as a plain fill of a dark shade of blue or a pleasant green or teal. (Just stay away from the yellow greens and the chartreuse popular in some circles but hardly enjoying universal appeal.)

Jim Endicott, presentations consultant, suggests using a Photoshop filter to add a bit of texture to the background. Then save the template in the compressed JPEG format, which can be shared by both Windows and Macintosh computers.[11]

Also, remember that what the template looks like on your computer monitor is no guarantee of how it will look on the LCD projection screen. Before you get too committed to a new template, make sure to give it the acid (LCD) test. I usually create a new template (background) and then add different typefaces in different sizes and different colors, plus a few bullets, lines, and boxes in colors that look good on my computer monitor. Then I put that collage of colors into a slide show and run it on my LCD projector in the daylight, with the shades open. The one time I failed to do that, I discovered in front of 500 people that red shows up better on my face than on a black-background slide.

3. Take the visual-learner approach and fill your screens with photographic images.

Photographs

I have three words for you: *Media Release Forms*. We all know there is nothing like children's faces to make a presentation come alive! But those same faces come with parents who can face you with a lawsuit. Especially in light of the horror stories about children with pictures on the Internet being approached and tracked down by unsavory characters, many parents are explicitly denying permission to take or use any photos or video footage of their children. If you take pictures of children in your classroom, I would consider seating children in such a way that the ones you cannot photograph are all on the same side of the room. Make sure you get a release form from the parents of every student or anyone else who

appears in one of your photographs.

Today, you might think you are just going to use the photo in a slide show you are presenting to the parents. Tomorrow, when that student has moved away from the district with no forwarding address—and you want to use that photograph in an article for *Educational Leadership* or the book ASCD has asked you to write—you are out of luck. That awesome image that captured the fire in children's eyes and jumped off the screen with its passionate joy of learning has to remain a memory in the scrapbook on your shelf. You can't publish it without permission.

As amateur photographers, how do we take *good photographs*? Even most professional photographers will tell you that out of every 24 pictures you shoot, you might get 3 or 4 really good ones. Don't be discouraged. Somehow, some days you capture exactly what you need. For example, look at the photo of a church spire.

The spire is perfect, but the picture has a few problems. What is that ugly splotch in the lower left-hand corner? The image is taller than it is wide, but the computer screen is just the opposite. Can this picture be saved?

It would take me a whole book just to describe what you can do with a program like Photoshop. There's so much, in fact, that many courts in the United States no longer accept photographs into evidence because of the alterations possible. Look at the church spire photo again. Here are the broad-level steps I took to edit the spire image for a slide show:

1. Scan the image.
2. Use Photoshop to crop and resize the photo, to achieve the right proportion and just keep the part of the photo that highlights the spire.
3. Adjust the image to saturate the colors (to show up better on the projected image) and increase the contrast so the image will be more striking when it's shown on the LCD projector.
4. Save the image in a format that the slide show can import (like JPEG).

The next photo shows the result.

Obviously, I'm having fun here salvaging and tweaking the image. But as you can imagine, in cases where images of people are involved, photo editing can tread on ethically thinner ice. For example, you can take an ex-boyfriend in a photograph of the two of you and darken his five-o'clock shadow to make him look sinister and evil. In the same photo, you can backlight yourself to create a subtle halo that would have just the opposite effect. By the way you set up and edit the shot, deliberately or inadvertently, you communicate your moral judgment of people in the photograph.

Apple Distinguished Educator Jerome Burg emphasizes this to students in his high school creative writing and satire classes. He points out, for example, that a close-up of a person's face reveals more of his or her character than a shot of that person taken from across the room. (As the *60 Minutes* interviewer asks his guest: "So, you lied under oath?" you can be sure the camera will zoom in on the guest's face.)

Projection Hardware

LCD Projectors

As I look into my liquid crystal ball, after a decade of working with Liquid Crystal Display (LCD) projection equipment, I feel confident in predicting that LCD projectors will find their way into more and more classrooms as they continue to approach what I call the *Model CLCB* (Cheaper, Lighter, Clearer, Brighter; see next page).

And, oh, yes, we'd also like great sound, inputs for two computers plus a VCR and a digital camera, a laser pointer built into the remote, a silent (but powerful) fan, zoom lens, and a three-year warranty.

Cheaper	≤ $3000
Lighter	≤ 5 pounds
Clearer	≥ XGA resolution
Brighter	≥ 3000 lumens

The amazing thing is that all of those ideal features *do* exist today, just not in one unit, at a price every classroom teacher can afford—the price in the chart.

To help other presenters and teachers make sense of all this, I have created a questionnaire that walks you through the selection criteria for an LCD projector (see chart, "Selecting an LCD Projector").

The evolving, updated version of this questionnaire is also posted on my portion of the Thornburg Center Web site (www.tcpd.org/burmark/burmark.html), under "Handouts."

If you want to send me your responses to these questions, I'd be happy to suggest some projectors you might want to consider. You don't have to copy the questions; just put the number of the question on the questionnaire plus your response in an e-mail to me: lynellb@aol.com.

To be realistic, consider the trade-offs:

- *For less money,* you get lower lumens (less brightness) and lower resolution (fewer pixels).
- *On the ultra lightweight units,* you sacrifice features like zoom lenses, powerful fans, two computer inputs, and so forth.
- *On the weight issue,* also be aware that the advertised weight typically does not include the cords and cables, remote, and carrying case, all of which could add up to another 4 to 5 pounds.

Selecting an LCD Projector

Dr. Lynell Burmark, Thornburg Center, lynellb@aol.com

Critical considerations:

1) How heavy a projector could you tolerate?
❑ ≥ 30 pounds   (Will it be mounted from the ceiling?)
❑ ≥ 24 pounds   (Will it stay in one lab or classroom?)
❑ 14 pounds   (Will it travel on a cart, classroom to classroom?)
❑ 8-13 pounds   (Will you carry it from room to room?)
❑ < 8 pounds   (Will you carry it to other buildings? In your car?)
❑ < 6 pounds   (Will you take it on airplanes?)

2) How many hours/day will it be used?
(This determines how rugged a projector you need, fan capability, etc.)

3) How bright a projector do you need?
What are the room lighting conditions? Please describe in detail. Are there windows without shades? Are there florescent lights? Do the lights run perpendicular or parallel to the screen? Can you turn off the lights in the third of the room closest to the screen? Does light from the windows shine directly on the screen? Are there high ceilings? Are the walls painted white? Is the room very, very light and bright? Do you need to present with the lights on? How large is the screen? How big is the room?

4) What resolution do you need?
Check the resolution of the monitor output on your computer. (Look under monitors and you'll see numbers like 800 x 600 or 1024 x 768.) You want to match the LCD resolution to that of your computer.
❑ 800 x 600   SVGA
❑ 1024 x 768   XGA
❑ 1280 x 1024   SXGA
❑ Higher resolution (bigger numbers), please specify.

5) What is your price range?
What would you like to spend?
What is the absolute most you can spend?

E-mail me your responses. If you wish, include a number where I can call you, and/or a mailing address where I can send you information (no charge to you).

Good News
Better models come out often and prices are always dropping. Contact me when you are ready to order. That way you'll have the best information when you need it.

Why do you need an LCD projector? Can't you just project your slides on the television already hanging in the corner or perched on the 200-pound media cart? It's an issue of visibility, and the answer depends on the number of viewers. The rule of thumb is that you take the diagonal measurement of the screen and divide by two. If you have a 35-inch television, a maximum of 17 to 18 people will be able to easily view its display.

When it comes to projected images, bigger is definitely better.

The Flexlab, Rear-Screen Projection

Especially for new installations, presentation rooms and classrooms should at least consider the option of rear screen projection. Staff at Stanford University's Meyer Library gave this a great deal of thought when upgrading their facility.

In their exemplary Flexible Class-Lab (see photo), they didn't want the equipment to dominate the classroom. They opted for setups where what you see in the classroom is an elegant 6' x 8' black mesh rectangle, flush with the wall.

What you don't see is the room behind the screen where the projector and reflection mirrors throw the image on to the backside of the screen. In the classroom in front of the screen, students plug laptops into floor outlets scattered under the flexible tables and between the beanbag chairs on the floor (see photo).

The students interact with each other, the professor, and the images on the screen, without even thinking about the technology. Professors from all departments access the online scheduler to sign up to use these facilities.

Note: A cart keeps the laptop computers and their network adapters conveniently available for use whenever needed during class sessions, and it allows the computers to be wheeled into a secure area when not in use. The instructor's presentation station can be easily moved to any place in the room. (For more images and information, visit the Stanford University Web site and search for "flexlab": http://rits.stanford.edu/).

A particularly powerful use of rear-screen projection technology would be in classrooms where students could prepare backdrops like stage settings for dramatic presentations they could act out in front of the screen. (You can't do that with front projection because the "actors" would create shadow figures whenever they stood between the projector and the screen.)

I visited an elementary school in Vancouver, Washington, with an interesting floor plan that lends itself to this kind of rear screen projection. As you enter the large double glass doors into the school, there is a 12-foot-wide entrance foyer. Directly ahead, in a 40' x 40' sunken area, is the media center with computers and production stations with scanners, document cameras, and other input devices. At the far end of this center is the stage with its screen flush against the back wall. I suggested that when the screen was not in use for instructional purposes, it could project the weekly winner of an electronic poster design contest, welcoming visitors to the school.

Into the Future

Flat-Screen Plasma Displays

An alternative to traditional and rear-projection screens is the flat-panel, plasma display. These luminescent beauties hang like landscape paintings on the wall. Unlike the typical television or CRT (cathode ray tube) computer monitor, they are only 3 to 4 inches deep, so they fit conveniently into relatively small spaces. They are starting to show up in corporate meeting rooms and in some private homes. The legendary Bill Gates purportedly uses dozens of them to create ambiance and project artwork to match the taste of particular visitors to his home.

Currently, the plasma displays have a few problems: a slight greenish tint to images, a price point that needs

taming, and a size (42-inch diagonal) that would make them inappropriate for audiences of more than 20 viewers. Still, this is a product worth keeping on your radar screen.

Lights, Camera, Action—In the "Palm" of Your Hand

As digital cameras become more affordable, schools are putting them in the hands of students and opening up all kinds of creative opportunities. Which assignment do you think would generate more interest?

- Write a research report on adolescent love.
- Videotape interviews with your high school classmates and create a video showing their opinions and concerns about love.

I've been particularly excited about using hand-held computers for capturing photographic quality images. The ubiquitous hand-held computers were not originally built to create and deliver electronic slides; but with the latest Kodak snap-on camera attachment, they are beginning to do just that. Executive Director of the Digital Exploration Society Robert L. Lindstrom predicts:

> We are already beginning to see palm-size computers that double as cell phones, fax machines and Web browsers. But just you wait. The portable tools we have today for capture, creation and delivery are only primitive precursors to the personal information appliances to come. In ten years, such devices will be part still and motion cameras capable of film-quality resolution and theater-quality sound recording. They will be as powerful as today's fastest business computers. They will uplink to satellites and download into any presentation display system.[12]

From the Classroom to the World

It took 50 years for overhead projectors to migrate from the bowling alley to the classroom. Let's hope that the journey for high-end presentation systems will be more rapid. Steelcase Corporation, already transforming corporate "Dilbert"-style cubicles into information theaters, could help us design more productive classrooms where every space is a presentation place. The warm, rich wood paneling along the front of the classroom could fade into King Ferdinand and Queen Isabella's throne room at the touch of a button. A student could have a live dialogue with the royals as he took on the role of Columbus. The bank of windows, looking over a virtual spring meadow, could open to the flooding banks of the Nile, as students studied farming in that community. With another button-click, they could be transported to Bangladesh, where similar floods annually cover much of the landscape. Today's news? The earthquake in India? The train wreck in London? The video-streaming CRT-side chat from the President of the United States? No problem. Excuse me for a moment, please, while I turn down the volume. . . .

The Digital Playground

OKAY, CLASS, IT'S TIME FOR A POP QUIZ, AND LET'S NOT ALWAYS see the same hands.

TRUE	FALSE	
		1. There is a tendency to think of visual images as less important, less "academic" than text.
		2. It's appropriate for kindergarten children to color a picture and then write a caption.
		3. By second or third grade, students use pencils more often than crayons.
		4. If you're having fun, you're not learning. (The "fun police" are watching, just in case.)

Answers: 1. True, 2. True, 3. True, 4. False

Question number four seems to score the most wrong answers. As the movie *Matilda* spelled out (see illustration). . . .

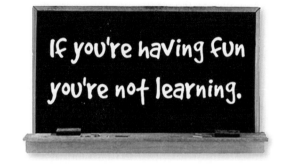

Even the term *schoolwork* implies that the goal is to make education as laborious as possible. And it isn't just in school. Our society (or at least the senior segment) believes that serious work means text. The last time my parents came to visit at my house, I was logging a 12-hour day on the Macintosh. My father could not understand how anyone could work that long on a computer. I left the room for a few minutes, and when the colorful "Fish" screen saver came on, I overheard him beckoning my mother: "Look, Mary! I told you she was playing!"

The beauty of computers is that they can make work *seem* like fun. And they definitely make it easier for teachers to incorporate fish or other visuals in their lessons. Before I had access to computers, I spent thousands of tedious hours manually cutting and pasting visuals, including over a hundred flash cards of high-frequency vocabulary antonyms. To make the cards big enough for the whole class to see, I had to cut three-inch-high letters out of black construction paper, glue them to yellow card stock, and then go to the district office to laminate the cards. Because I was teaching French as well as English as a second language, I had to make two sets of the cards (see photo).

New Clicks on Old Tricks

Today, I can open a slide show program and create a hundred "flash cards" in an hour. For example, for a lesson on *antonyms*, thanks to the power of technology, instead of turning the card over for the "opposite" word, I just "dissolve" to a second slide with both words on it (see "up/down" illustration).

Even though this is basically a vocabulary drill, it feels like a game as students are engaged in "guessing" the opposite word. Also, by connecting pairs of information, this game is actually a *mnemonic* device. As any advertiser can tell you, the best way to make sure you remember their product is to attach that product or their company name to a compelling visual image (often from the "lifestyles of the rich and famous" collection). This is why celebrities are so effective and highly paid as spokespersons.

Teachers need to be at least as shrewd as advertisers. When we introduce vocabulary words, spelling lists, or glossaries, instead of sterile and decontextualized alphabetical lists, we can improve comprehension and retention by introducing the words in meaningful contexts. Knowing that the brain thrives on connecting *up* with *down*, we can take a time-tested method like flash cards and do it better with technology. Knowing that students learn better when they construct their own knowledge, we can have teams of students create the slide shows of these antonym pairs (or any other pairs of information) and then ask each group to present their "game" for the rest of the class to play.

Sequencing

The Joke

Every day, take the most tedious thing you have to convey that day and imagine a digital-visual way to make it engaging and fun. For example, for a free-flowing, nonlinear person like myself, grammar and syntax fall into the mind-numbingly boring category. So how would I teach paragraph construction and topic sentences? Remember, this lesson has to bring tears (of laughter) to the eyes of the students. It also has to keep me awake. (I actually did fall asleep once while teaching a French grammar lesson. Fortunately, the blackboard broke my fall, so no one was hurt.)

I would start the class by saying: "I just heard this great new joke. Want to hear it?" Then I would proceed to tell the joke with great enthusiasm, but with the lines all mixed up.[1] The punch line would be somewhere in the middle and the last line wouldn't be funny at all. At that point, I would break out laughing (good for *my* immune system) and look totally puzzled that *they* didn't get it. I'd repeat the last line (not funny) and laugh some more. When I had a good enough chortle, I would flick on the LCD projector, with the mixed up joke typed on the screen.

I'd wait a few seconds to see if some bright student would realize that rearranging the sentences could vastly improve the joke. If they were too busy worrying about my apparent loss of sanity, I'd go ahead and move the first sentence and ask if maybe that helped. Students could volunteer to move the remaining sentences.

Then I'd divide the class into groups of three to five students and have each group write and scramble a joke. Their team joke would be graded on the following criteria:

0–10 points   Correct punctuation, grammar, spelling, and syntax; expressive and proper use of language

0–10 points   Positive humor (no off-color jokes, racial or ethnic slurs, or putting people down)

0–10 points   Legible, attractive presentation and enthusiastic delivery

The team grade would be calculated by *multiplying* the three scores above. Any bad words (inappropriate language) or negative humor would result in zero points for that category and hence zero points for the total grade.

Besides this activity adding to my growing joke collection, students would have a good time and prove experientially the upgraded adage: "If you're having fun, you're probably learning."

I'll Take Mine Scrambled

Jokes and eggs aren't the only things you can scramble. Other possibilities might include poems, songs, or other routines, as the table shows.

The morning routine	Get dressed, take a shower, get out of bed, etc. (good for drilling reflexive verbs in French)
Sections of short stories	Three Bears and their chairs (lots of repetition for beginning or early language learners)
Stanzas of poems or songs	Especially lines that rhyme (popular songs are great motivators; or try imagist poems)
Steps in a recipe	This is especially fun if one person gives instructions for another to follow—literally.

Calendars

Another kind of sequencing is creating calendars. At St. Joseph's School, classroom teacher Jane Gerlich has her 22 second graders creating calendars of recipes to give their mothers for Mother's Day. The students actually prepared the dishes and took photos that they scanned into the computer. The unedited recipes provide the children's explanations of how to prepare the various delicacies, such as Jell-O. Emily supplied an interesting recipe (see illustrations).

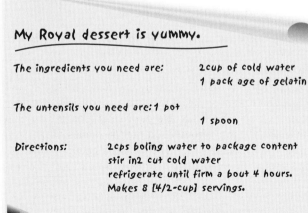

My Royal dessert is yummy.

The ingredients you need are: 2 cup of cold water
                                 1 pack age of gelatin

The untensils you need are: 1 pot
                                 1 spoon

Directions: 2cps boling water to package content
               stir in2 cut cold water
               refrigerate until firm a bout 4 hours.
               Makes 8 [4/2-cup] servings.

               Strawberry banana jello is my favorite.

Other calendar ideas, made possible—even easy—by computers, the Internet, scanners, digital cameras, and color printers, might include the following:

- Scenes from the neighborhood (get a local realtor to sponsor the printing).

- Rooms in a local museum, historical mansion, or government building (possibly combined with a tour or open house where the calendars could be sold or sponsored by a patron).

- Animals, flowers, mountains, or images in Pics4Learning[2] themed collections (a tutorial on calendar-making is also posted on that site).

- Any topic that you are studying (Civil War, monuments of France, etc.).

- Fine art (from the Web Museum) with paintings chosen to reflect the weather (e.g., Gustave Caillebotte's *Paris: A Rainy Day*, and *Rooftops Under Snow*; van Gogh's *Orchard with Blossoming Plum Trees*), or just favorite paintings from a particular artist.

Storyboarding

Especially for young children, any kind of visual sequencing activity helps train them to read. One of my favorite software programs from the Edmark-Riverdeep Corporation, Millie & Bailey Kindergarten, has an activity where students "Make a Movie." They rearrange a sequence of three or four frames and then tell the projectionist to roll the film: Lights, camera, action!

Cinematographers refer to this movie-making process as "storyboarding." The flow of the action and the story line are mapped out as a sequence of thumbnail images representing scenes in the show. Programs like Power-Point make it easy to reorder thumbnails in the slide view mode.

Apple Distinguished Educator Jerome Burg asks students in high school English classes at Granada High School (Livermore, California) to do a variation on this process. Teams of students pick one of several novels to read and then reduce each chapter down to four cartoon panels. They discuss issues of plot, character development, and critical action and argue about which elements must be drawn for someone who has not read the book to be able to follow the story. (Contrast this intriguing strategy to students' reading the book individually and answering multiple-choice questions at the end of each chapter.)

Burg asks the students: "What do you think the author wanted you to see in your mind's eye? That is what you need to draw." Research on the Internet about Baroque France, for example, gave the students the detail they needed to draw the costumes and room decor for *Cyrano de Bergerac*.

When drawing cartoons, students must also choose the words (to go in the voice balloons) that reveal the character's emotions, motives, and personality. Every element in this shorthand account of the novel has to communicate volumes (see Cyrano cartoon).

A Constructivist Approach

The beauty of storyboarding novels and plays is that the transformed works are created by the students. Clearly, they start with the author's ideas, but they end up by building their own masterpieces. There is a sense of

accomplishment and a pride of ownership as they produce something new, something that speaks to them personally.

Lessons developed around this kind of process will be the home runs of any teacher's career.

The Streets of Sunnyvale

As part of a lesson I had developed called *From Images to Words*, I commissioned colleague-photographer Lou Fournier to shoot photographs of beautiful autumnal scenery near my home in Sunnyvale, California. I selected 16 photos and scanned them into a PowerPoint presentation. I also made six sets of photographs and labeled the backs of those photos with the file names of the images. Initially, I was going to share a poem I had written about the scenes, "The Streets of Sunnyvale," but I decided against it for fear it might be perceived as "the right answer" and stifle rather than inspire creativity.

The first two times I used the lesson was with educators during a workshop on *Multimedia and Multiple*

The Streets of Sunnyvale

I love the streets of Sunnyvale
Especially in the fall,
When trees are dressed so splendidly
For our autumnal ball.

The birches rain their golden leaves
By maples crimson red.
Persimmons perch on graceful limbs
While ducks quack to be fed.

Church towers, crosses, roofs and spires
Reach high above the town,
As power lines stretch 'cross the sky
And gnarly trees turn brown.

Remember in the Golden State
Some trees aren't gold at all.
Two rows of palm trees join the dance
And stay to end the ball.

Intelligences at a Florida Educational Technology Conference. I had attendees divide into four groups of six. Each group received a packet of 16 photos with the instruction to spread them out on the table and to put them into an order that suggested a story or poem. Once they had the order determined, they were to copy down the file names (numbering them 1–16) and bring them to me so I could reorder the slides and save that presentation under their group name.

Then each group came to the front and presented their original creations using the computer and LCD projector. Because I had trees with autumn leaves in some slides and palm trees in others, several groups assumed there was a journey involved. One group traveled from their home in Maine to visit Grandma in Florida. Another group focused on the church cross and spire and made a spiritual journey of discovery. No two presentations were alike. The groups marveled at their own creativity and at how each presentation was exquisite in its own way.

As part of the workshop, I gave each participant a compact disc (CD) with the images on it, so they could try the activity back in their own schools.

Earl the Squirrel

As most educators know, what works with adults does not necessarily work with children. (I'll share more on that account later in this chapter.) I thought 4th graders would be an interesting age group to try Sunnyvale photos because they would be able to write independently. Quite conveniently, Wes Burmark is an award-winning 4th grade teacher. Always willing to do his baby sister a favor, "Mr. B." loaded the PowerPoint slides onto his classroom computers. He decided just to give the students 9 or 10 images each, instead of the 16 given to the adults. The students already knew how to drag and drop slides in the slide view and to type text onto the slides.

He instructed the students to

- Include at least five members on their team.
- Put the pictures in order and write a story.
- Rearrange the slides on the computer to match their story.
- Present their slide show to the class.

In Wes's classroom at Crescent Heights Elementary School (in Tacoma, Washington), there are six Macintosh computers along the back wall of the classroom. Students had an hour to plan their stories on one day and another hour to work on the computers and rehearse their presentations the next day.

Earl the Squirrel

One day Earl the squirrel came down a tree.	He found some ducks who told him about the peaches.	Earl climbed up the peach tree and threw the peaches down.
He jumped to a nearby tree.	He slipped and fell into a car through the open sunroof.	The ducks jumped in after him.
Earl started the car, and drove down the road.	They came to the house that Earl got kicked out of.	He found his old tree and partied with the ducks!

One of their presentations featured a new character, Earl the Squirrel (see illustration). The team[3] actually typed their story lines onto each frame. In the interest of legibility for these thumbnails, I moved the captions below each picture. Wes Burmark also developed a rubric for students to evaluate their experience (see chart).

Every Picture Tells A Story

Type Y for yes. Type N for no.

Rate yourself:
__ I helped put the pictures in order to create our story.
__ I wrote a portion of the story.
__ I helped revise.
__ I took part in the technology portion of our story.
__ I took part in the presentation.

Rate your group:
__ People in my group let me participate.
__ People in my group helped me.
__ People in my group made me feel important.
__ Everyone in the group did a portion of the work.

Additional comments:_____

_____

Constructing Your Own Slide Show

After doing the initial project with my photos, students would probably enjoy collecting their own images. If you wanted them to do a multimedia presentation on their neighborhood (*The Streets of Tacoma*, for example), you could ask them to think about how the landscapes of their city affect how they feel about where they live.

In teams of five or six, the students could take photos of their neighborhood with an eye to the natural elements and how they contribute beauty to the cityscape. I would admit to the students that I had to shoot three rolls of 24-exposure film to get the 16 images I shared with them. Brainstorm a list of criteria for a good photograph and have students use this rubric for taking and then selecting their best photos. Depending on the story they want to write, they may want people in the scenes, they may want close ups, panoramic shots, different perspectives, and so on. Make sure the students notice that in order to fill the computer screen with the image, the photos need to be taken in the landscape/horizontal rather than the portrait/vertical orientation. They should also think about the emotion they want to express, and how to select and frame images to convey those feelings.

As they work through the "dialogue" between the images and the words and determine the "story line" through sequencing the images, students will generate richer language and more personally meaningful prose or poetry than they could by typing words on a blank page.

Once the slide shows are assembled, have the students practice the delivery and coach each other on dramatic effect. Encourage them to use complementary background music, costumes, and props, as appropriate, to convey the mood. If possible, plan to videotape the presentations.

Variations on a Theme

The slide shows or presentations can take on a life of their own, in many ways:

- An interesting twist to the project would be to have each team scramble their slides and give them to

another group to interpret. The presentations could then occur in a round-robin fashion (see chart).

Images From	
Group A	Group B makes presentation, then Group A makes presentation.
Group B	Group C makes presentation, then Group B makes presentation.
Group C	Group D makes presentation, then Group C makes presentation.
Group D	Group A makes presentation, then Group D makes presentation.

- Invite the class members to give feedback, telling each group what they liked about their images, story, and presentation delivery. How did the presentation make them feel? Did they want to visit the places in the photos? Did they share the sentiments expressed in the poem or story?

  Ask the class to discuss how it felt when another group presented their images. How did they feel about presenting their own images versus those from another group? Which was more interesting?

- Consider collecting all their stories or poems into an anthology to print out or publish on the Web.

- Have the students select their favorite (most meaningful) image from each poem or story and then have the class as a whole select 12 images to publish as a calendar to use as a school fundraiser. (With the "Images of the City" theme, the students might be able to find a local bank, real estate agency, or even the Chamber of Commerce to sponsor the printing of the calendars.)

- For the musically inclined, suggest that the poems be put to music and that they be delivered to the class as recordings or live performances (with the slide show images in the background).

- For the technically inclined, suggest that, where appropriate in the slide show, they include

    - sounds (of nature)
    - video clips
    - links to relevant Web sites

- Have students interview older adults in the community and write about the neighborhood or the city from their perspective. If they have old family photos that could be copied and scanned for the presentation, that would add to the sharing and understanding.

- Where there is access to a digital camcorder, these community interviews (as well as the delivery of the final poetry presentations) can be recorded. Then students can create desktop movies to show to family members and include as video clips on the class or school Web site.

Other Writing Projects to Prepare Students for the Real World

These types of projects take a *constructivist* approach to learning: students produce (or select, edit, and arrange) images and write their own scripts. Although the basic requirements are well defined, such projects are quite open-ended, encouraging students to push the technical, artistic, linguistic, dramatic, and musical elements of their work.

The use of student-created images (photos, videos) as the first step in the writing process can be applied to prose, travel logs, short stories, research reports, mock advertisements, and a variety of other writing genres. The juxtaposition of slide shows and live dramatic performances prepares students for "real life" employment where one is frequently called on to present persuasive arguments or sell a product or service concept. Group teamwork is a critical workplace skill, particularly in this kind of creative process. Finally, the combination of word processing, presentation software, and Web-based research is a staple for most projects in higher education and the workplace.

Early success in writing and self expression will encourage students to take more creative risks and to have more confidence in their own original work and ideas rather than seeing schoolwork as the tedious job of cutting and pasting other people's work (with attribution, of course).

Another Point of View

Another Page

With computers now including CD burners, it's a simple matter for students to create graphics-heavy projects on CDs. One such project, *Another page, lost in thought*, was a multimedia experience developed by Jerome Burg's creative writing students at Granada High School in Livermore, California. A group of students designed the template to be used for each page, and one student (who discovered his talent for photography through this project)[4] took pictures of each of the students. Students each wrote a poem and recorded it for the CD.

another page
lost in thought   *jessica cooper*
to john

Sitting in the corner, I cry.
Hoping you're not where I think.
Where I know.
Who stands before you?
Friend or foe?
Is it hate in his eyes? or fear?
Will he hit you with his fist?
Or his bullet?

another page
lost in thought   *steve palmer*

In memory of those who died
in the holocaust.
A pile of shoes.
All of the people.
The time lost.
The time set back.
The eyes are gone.
The wishes known.
Now they will travel
No shoes at all.

Another Time

In his poem about the pile of shoes from Nazi concentration camp victims, student Steve Palmer reveals how deeply he had been moved by seeing that exhibit[5] at the Auschwitz Museum the year before. The pile of shoes shown in the photo represents one day's collection at the peak of the gassings, about 25,000 pairs.

For students studying World War II or novels describing the Nazi atrocities, logging onto the Cybrary of the

Holocaust (http://www.remember.org) will make the experience much more real. Watching movies like *Schindler's List* and *Life Is Beautiful* can also deepen the students' understanding. If students have time in a lab with a high-speed Internet connection, encourage them to conduct further research, typing words such as "Auschwitz," "Holocaust," or "concentration camps" into their favorite search engines. Read the touching article in the May 2000 issue of *Learning & Leading with Technology*, about teaching *Night* by Elie Wiesel using the Internet.[6] The authors suggest that the teacher walk around the lab to encourage and react to the students' discoveries. They also recommend using Bette Midler's recording of "From a Distance," as well as the video of Elie Wiesel speaking about the experiences he describes in the book.

Another Perspective

Using primary sources to investigate historical events, students can draw their own conclusions as to the issues behind the political conflicts. For example, check the

National Archives and Records Administration Web site (http://www.nara.gov) study on wartime powers of persuasion:

> Persuading the American public became a wartime industry, almost as important as the manufacturing of bullets and planes. The government launched an aggressive propaganda campaign to galvanize public support, and some of the nation's foremost intellectuals, artists, and filmmakers became warriors on that front.

The NARA online exhibit of World War II poster art features 33 posters and one sound file from a more extensive exhibit that was presented in the National Archives Building in Washington, D.C., from May 1994 to February 1995. Like the original, this exhibit is divided into two parts, which represent two psychological approaches used in rallying public support for the war (see illustrations).

St. Joseph's middle school history teacher Dennis Hill uses the media literacy lessons from the Just Think Foundation[7] to introduce the study of World War II. Using an LCD projector, he shows a few of these propaganda posters to the class while discussing the role of artists in mobilizing resources for the war effort. He helps the students look at the "motivation" behind the messages. Then each student picks a topic to research, such as one of the following:

- Recruitment (women)
- Recruitment (men)
- Increased farm and weapons production
- Rosie the Riveter
- Anti-German or anti-Japanese propaganda
- Segregation of American troops
- Bond promotions (raising money for the war)
- Conservation of resources, rationing
- Jewish prisoners (at Treblinka) forced by the Nazis to develop German propaganda posters
- The psychology of fear

To illustrate their topic, each student assembles a four-slide PowerPoint presentation (three posters taken from the actual WWII collection plus one original creation). Pretending to be "propaganda artists," the students explain the color, symbols, and purpose of the posters to the rest of the class.

Groups of three students then collaborate to make illustrated reports on related social issues, such as these:

- The changing role of women on the home front (who took jobs traditionally held by men) during the war and the long-term effect on U.S. postwar society.
- The role of black soldiers (based on firsthand

accounts written by men who served in the segregated units).

- The kind of battle they would be willing to give their lives for today. (Who are the enemies of the United States since the end of the Cold War?)

Time Machines

Not only the young marine in Da Nang, Vietnam (see photo), but also immigrants arriving at Ellis Island . . . the Wright Brothers flying . . . men constructing the Empire State Building . . . a Depression-era soup line . . . Omaha Beach . . . the mushroom cloud . . . Lyndon Johnson taking the Presidential oath . . . footprints on the Moon . . . war in the Persian Gulf . . . . All these are in the National Archives exhibition of the 20th century.

This exhibition beckons us to

- Look back in history, freeze a moment in time, and imagine ourselves as part of the past.
- See how famous and ordinary folk appeared in both posed and unguarded moments.
- Relive great events and everyday life in exquisite detail.
- Learn how people dressed and carried themselves, and sometimes even judge their moods or guess their thoughts.[8]

Using an LCD projector to display one of these striking photographs, such as that of the young marine, as students come into class is an extremely effective way of getting them to settle down quickly and focus on the lesson for the day. Take a few moments for them to study the image and write in their journals (or type into their handheld computers) what they think it signifies. Then highlight some key facts and offer a starting point where students can begin further research.

In Black and White

One initial problem for students viewing old photographs is that they aren't used to seeing images in black and white. Remember, this is the *USA Today* generation. A teacher friend of mine was watching a black-and-white movie on television with his 8-year-old son. A few moments into the film, the boy asked: "Were people that color back then?"

It might be worth a quick virtual trip to the American Museum of Photography to put black and white versus color in a realistic context.[9] While you're there, take a moment to visit the daguerreotypes of Southworth and Hawes. Their world seems light years away from the disposable and mega-pixel digital cameras our children get in their Christmas stockings.

Another Space

After an exhilarating voyage through time, we might as well take a trip through space. I already mentioned the Astronomy Picture of the Day, which is part of NASA's efforts to share resources with the public.

The striking photo of a "sunpillar" was taken by Stan Richard. The explanation of how the ice crystals form and reflect the sun's light can be found in the Astronomy Picture of the Day archive for March 13, 2001.[10]

Several science teachers, as well as elementary school classroom teachers, are starting the period or the school day with one of these images. Again, let the students reflect and speculate before sharing the information provided by the NASA scientists. Teachers may also want to take advantage of other programs and curriculum support materials on the NASA education web site.[11]

You can never start too young with preparing the next generation of scientists. St. Joseph's School kinder-

garten teacher Kathy Cleveland has developed a video-pals project with kindergarten teacher Barbara Vandenberg, from Spanish River Christian School in Boca Raton, about half an hour away. Each week, Cleveland videotapes her little e-scientists as they respond to questions from their remote colleagues and send back questions of their own. They are much more motivated to conduct the "scientific research" when they know they have an audience waiting for the results. The first video was used to introduce the scientists to each other.

The two kindergarten classes plan to meet face to face for a picnic halfway between the two schools sometime in the spring. They will definitely take advantage of video conferencing for live, real-time dialogue as soon as the equipment is available at the school sites.

Another Country, Language, and Culture

Of course, the teachers and students most excited about "the next killer app" (video conferencing) are in the foreign-language classrooms. Instead of the traditional pen pals (or e-mail buddies) sending written text back and forth in the "target language," they'll be able to sit across the table from Pierre and Monique and have real-time conversation in French.

Most price-conscious K–12 educators are still just dreaming about video conferencing. As usual, we wait. We ask the government to pay for a little more research, we watch for the critical mass of business users to bring the price down, and we rely on higher education to work the last few bugs out. Even so, I suspect it won't be long until the hardware is free with a year's service subscription.

In the meantime, Web "visits" to another country are already a tremendous resource. St. Joseph's Spanish teacher Daryl Yianna asks her students to create Power-Point travel brochures that illustrate why tourists would want to come to the Spanish-speaking country they are featuring. In the process of learning about the particular country, students also discover the importance of selecting just the right image. Do you show the slums or just the white sandy beaches? The government buildings or curbside cafes? Images with people having fun or peaceful landscapes with no people? Close-ups or vista views? What does "truth in advertising" mean?

When it came to *presenting* the slide shows, students quickly discovered the effect of visuals. As Alex wrote on his project evaluation: "When you read a regular report, people just listen and learn. With an electronic presentation, people learn, read, listen, watch, and applaud!"

Combining Real and Virtual Worlds

Museum "Trips"

In anticipation of the class visit to an Impressionist exhibition at the Norton Museum of Art in West Palm Beach,

Florida, St. Joseph's middle school French teacher Kristen Carley created an online Treasure Hunt. Students "visited" the Web Museum to uncover interesting facts about Claude Monet and other painters of the Impressionist era. They looked for warm and cool colors and for the moods and feelings evoked by different paintings.

Similarly, online research of Florida's railroads was enhanced by a field trip to the Flagler Museum[12] by students in Michele Fritts's 4th grade class. The challenge was to collect all the students' research on the Flaglers, the building of the railroads, and the change in South Florida economy—and edit it into a coherent "story" that could be scripted, digitized, and shared as an electronic presentation for parents and the community. Discussing the effect and the message of each image helped students—even at this early age—with visual literacy, as well as communication and presentation skills.

Many of the museums with online collections are also providing educational materials and study guides, as well as multimedia previews for classes planning to visit the actual museums. Be sure to avail yourself of these materials, and also consider sharing with the museum the materials your classes create.

From Sea to Shining Sea!

Many online photo galleries are of such excellent quality that they seem to transport you to the scenes they are depicting. The high-resolution images from the National Oceanic and Atmospheric Administration's (NOAA) online photo gallery,[13] for example, are some of the best I've seen.

Students will love the tornado pictures, the ship collections, and the undersea explorations from the shallow coastlines to the depths of the ocean's abyss. Younger students, especially, will be drawn to "NOAA's Ark," with its collection of marine mammal photos—"a virtual boatload of fins, fur, and feathers." Also plan to visit the coral kingdoms of the Pacific and the Caribbean, and America's coastlines—from "sea to shining sea."

Sun, Moon, and Stars

Is it time for religious studies, character education, or a few quiet moments of introspection? Don't miss the "Beginnings and Endings"[14] Web site with its breathtaking sunrises, sunsets, moonbeams, and moonlight. For example, take a moment to savor the sky captured by Commander John Bortniak, NOAA Corps (retired) (see photo).

Little Eugene must have been looking at this kind of sky when he wrote his letter (see illustration). Eugene takes us to the heart of visual literacy. It's not just looking at pretty pictures. It's understanding how we connect those pictures to what we already know about the world,

Dear God,

I didn't think orange went with purple until I saw the sunset you made on Tuesday. That was cool.

— Eugene

life, relationships, and values—and then making sense of our expanded world.

> **I didn't think . . . until I saw.**
> —Eugene

Personal Experience and Interpretation of Images

> **We look at the world and see what we have learned to believe is there.**
> —Aaron Siskind (photographer)

I have researched, written, and preached about the power of images and the importance of first impressions. Colleagues have dared me to show up for a conference keynote dressed outrageously and to deliver (or at least start delivering) my presentation with a straight face. At the moment, I'm still waiting for exactly the right occasion.

In the meantime, I decided to run a little experiment with students. Two brave colleagues, Jennifer Fuentes (St. Joseph's) and Jerome Burg (Granada High School), agreed to help me out. Without identifying me, they showed the photo (in color) on this page to a group of students and asked them to write down what they thought of the person. How old is she? What does she do for a living? What kind of person do you think she is? What is she thinking? What else can you tell about her from the photo?

In full color, with the hot pink hat and hair and the big turquoise sunglasses, this photo made quite an impression on the students, as follows:

The high schoolers:

This person seems happy. She looks like she would get along with kids. She would be able to connect with

them and understand them. Maybe she is a kindergarten teacher or a counselor at children's hospitals. She might even be a nurse who truly cares about her patients. I don't think a need for money plays a great role in her life. She likes to sing karaoke.   —Eva

This lady is one of those 40–45-year-old women who likes to pretend she's 20. She probably has teenage daughters and borrows their clothes all of the time. Her name is Kathy and she just quit her high-paying office job to become a nightclub singer so that she can act younger and have some spontaneity and adventure in her life. She smokes, which is why her teeth are yellow and her skin is wrinkled.   —Lindsay

This woman grew up in a middle to upper class society because she has straight teeth, meaning when she was younger she had braces. Her real age is of no importance. She is young at heart; you can tell by the smile. Material possessions aren't of any value because she isn't wearing any jewelry. That and she probably spends a lot of time around children who like to pull on necklaces and earrings. She has light brown hair that she doesn't feel she needs to dye, despite incoming gray hairs. She is comfortable with who she is.
          —Liz

The middle schoolers:

This lady is 45 years old. She is an undercover FBI agent. She is a nice person but could be different in her disguises. She is probably thinking about how she can see who is going to steal the Mona Lisa painting.
          —Trevor

I think she is about 40 years old. She looks like she is a mom and does not go to work. She looks fun and probably is fun to be around. She looks like she is laughing about a joke or something. The pink hair makes her look like she just got back from a party.

—Paige

I think that this lady is in her mid to late 40s. She looks like a shoe designer. She seems like a really silly person and she designs really strange shoes. I don't think that she would like this picture of herself.

—Katie

From this small sample, you realize how different people looking at the same picture saw a wildly different person behind the sunglasses. Who I really am (a nonsmoker whose parents could not afford braces) was not the issue. What was going on in the students' lives (and their mothers') clearly influenced their view of the photograph.

The Vision to Create a World

What our students see—on television, at the movies, in their video games, and in the daily drama of life with friends and family—creates a world vision that colors their interpretation of any and all additional visual input. As we expose students to new images—to images of truth and beauty, courage and compassion, achievement and hope—we can expand their understanding not only of our subject matter, but also of the choices they can make in life.

"I Have a Dream"

Who can forget Martin Luther King Jr.'s famous "I Have a Dream" speech?[15] One of the things that made it so powerful was the *vision* he conveyed of people of all races living, working, and playing together. When you heard him speak, you *saw* what he envisioned.

When we experience visions, daydreams, nightmares, spiritual revelations, poignant memories, "Aha!" moments, or even delightful flights of imagination, they tend to come to us in images rather than words, most often as a kind of cinema that combines dialogue and images into action sequences. As my colleague Lou Fournier says, "Imagery is the language of the spirit," by which he means that an image bypasses linguistic and rational hurdles and imparts meaning immediately and viscerally. As with Rorschach tests and as seen in the simple photograph interpretation exercise we conducted with middle and high schoolers, images all around us induce deeply personal perspectives and highly *affective* projections. Visual literacy is about understanding how and why such projections work and how we can affect an audience clearly, responsibly, and purposefully.

One night when I fell into bed too tired to even change into my nightclothes, my husband asked: "Why are you coming to bed with your glasses on?" Even exhausted, I couldn't let him have the last word, so I retorted: "In case I have to read something in my dreams." Of course, I have yet to read anything in my dreams. The visions are sometimes *still* images, more often full-motion video, revealing truths and ideas to my mind's eye that my literal eyes were too busy to notice during the day. Studying those images takes us to a form of "visionary literacy," which is beyond the scope of this book, but too important not to at least mention as a concept to ponder.

Eyeglasses for the Mind

I think of "visual literacy" as 3–D eyeglasses for the mind. They are the lenses through which we see the meaning—the words and ideas—behind the images.

When we teach our students to view images—everything from universal symbols like the stick figures on public restroom doors to artfully composed professional photographs—we are guiding them through a visual experience that takes us beyond the two dimensions of the medium itself.

Learning to articulate the real-life experiences behind photos we cherish, extracting the "storyboards" from plays, poems, and novels, students can begin to read images and words with new eyes. They can embark on travel in both directions—from pictures to words and words to pictures—and be enriched by both the outbound and the return journey.

Center Stage

After completing projects such as those we've discussed in this book, students will

- Be able to use images as inspiration for more descriptive vocabulary and "imagery" in their writing.
- Be able to design purposeful communication using words and images.
- Have begun to develop a "voice."

- Have gained confidence and skill in their abilities to work in groups and contribute to a common goal.[16]

Why not harness the power of visual images to teach students to read and write and to comprehend and communicate content across the curriculum? Why not teach visual literacy as a means of preparing students for a life where a primary vehicle for communication (the Internet) is based on a graphical interface and where the value of a business is reflected in the quality of its visual representation? Why not take a more visual, project-based, and constructivist approach to education, and encourage students to illustrate, demonstrate, and celebrate what they learn in their own creative ways, rather than regurgitating irrelevant, decontextualized facts on impersonal, institutionalized, standardized tests?

It's time to let students' values, feelings, and achievements take center stage.

Traditional instructional practices cannot compete with MTV. But educators have the advantage—and the opportunity—to involve students in the creation and presentation of their own knowledge. By teaching students to use multimedia to express themselves, we can make our students stars, and our classrooms *center stage* for learning. Sit back and relax. The show is about to begin.

▶ Endnotes

Note: World Wide Web sites referenced in this book may have changed location or been discontinued since its publication. The author has made every effort to use active sites.

Chapter 1

1. Burns, P. T. *The Complete History of the Discovery of Cinematography* (Chapter 15: 1895–1900). Toronto: Author, 2001. [Online book]. Available: http://www.precinemahistory.net/1895.htm

2. *American Cinema*, PBS University, summer 2000.

3. Ibid.

4. Dunn, Judy L. "Television Watchers." *Instructor* 103, no. 8 (April 1994): 50–54.

5. Christopherson, Jerry T. "The Growing Need for Visual Literacy at the University." In *VisionQuest: Journeys Toward Visual Literacy.* Edited by Robert E. Griffin, J. M. Hunter, C. B. Schiffman, and W. J. Gibbs. University Park, PA: International Visual Literacy Association, 1997, pp. 169–174.

6. Heuston, Dustin. Waterford Institute, Provo, Utah, interviewed May 1999.

7. Schmitt, Maribeth C. "Lawmakers can make a difference for Indiana children." *Indiana Editorial Pages* (March 19, 1997) [Online]. Available: http://news.uns.purdue.edu/UNS/hot .topics/970318.Schmitt.html

8. National Science and Technology Council. *Ensuring a Strong U.S. Scientific, Technical, and Engineering Workforce in the 21st Century.* Washington, DC: National Science and Technology Council, 2000. Available: http://www.ostp.gov/html/workforcerpt.pdf

9. Council on Competitiveness. *Winning the Skills Race.* Washington, DC: Council on Competitiveness, U.S. Department of Commerce, 2000. Available: http://www.compete.org/news/news_index.html

10. Ibid.

11. U.S. Department of Labor. *Report on the American Workforce, 1999.* Washington, DC: U.S. Department of Labor, 2000. Available: http://stats.bls.gov/opub/rtaw/rtawhome.htm

12. Ibid.

13. 3M Corporation research cited in "Polishing Your Presentation." *3M Meeting Network Articles & Advice* (2001) [Online Article]. Available: http://www.3m.com/meetingnetwork/readingroom/meetingguide_pres.html

14. Simons, Tad. "Multimedia or bust?" (research by Dr. Hayward Andres and Dr. Candace Peterson), *Presentations* 7, (March 2000): 48-50.

15. Ganzel, Rebecca. "Power Pointless." *Presentations* (February 2000): 53-58. Available: http://www.presentations.com/techno/soft/2000/02/29_f2_ppl.html

16. Lindstrom, Robert L. "Visual Communications @ Work," Special Advertising Supplement to *Business Week*, July 31, 2000.

17. Hernandez-Ramos, Pedro. Business Development Manager, Worldwide Education, Cisco Systems, Inc., Milpitas, California, interviewed May 2000.

18. Nielson, Jakob. "Top Ten Mistakes in Web Page Design" (2001). [Online Article]. Available: http://www.useit.com/alertbox/9605.html

19. Trager, Louis, "Fireclick lights up page views." ZDNet: Inter@ctive Week News (February 28, 2000). [Online Article]. Available: http://www.zdnet.com/intweek/stories/news/0,4164,2449698,00.html

Chapter 2

1. Eco, Umberto. *A Theory of Semiotics*. Bloomington: Indiana University Press, 1979.

2. Postman, Neil. *Technopoly: The Surrender of Culture to Technology*. New York: Vintage Books, 1993.

3. Postman, Neil. *The End of Education: Redefining the Value of School*. New York: Knopf, 1996.

4. Meredith, Geoffrey. "The Demise of Writing." *The Futurist* 33, no. 8 (October 1999): 27-30.

5. "Numbers." *Time* 155, no. 6 (February 14, 2000): 25.

6. "Periscope," *Newsweek* (April 2, 2001): 9.

7. Gardner, Howard. *Frames of Mind*. New York: Basic Books, 1983.

8. Pavio, Allan. *Mental Representations: A Dual Coding Approach*. New York: Oxford University Press, 1986.

9. Rakes, Glenda C. "Teaching Visual Literacy in a Multimedia Age." *TechTrends* 43 (September 1999):14-15.

10. Levie, W. H., and Lentz, R. "Effects of Text Illustrations: A Review of Research." *Educational Communication and Technology Journal* 30, no. 4 (1982): 195–232.

11. Lindstrom, Robert L. "Being Visual: The Emerging Visual Enterprise." *Business Week* (April 19, 1999): Special Advertising Section.

12. 3M Corporation research cited in "Polishing Your Presentation." *3M Meeting Network Articles & Advice* (2001). [Online Article]. Available: http://www.3m.com/meetingnetwork/readingroom/meetingguide_pres.html

13. Hanke, Jon. "The Psychology of Presentation Visuals." *Presentations* (May 1998) [Online Article]. Available: http://www.presentations.com/deliver/audience/1998/05/13_f1_psy_01.html

14. 3M Corporation research cited in "The Power of Color in Presentations." *3M Meeting Network Articles & Advice* (2001) [Online Article]. Available: http://www.3m.com/meetingnetwork/readingroom/meetingguide_power_color.html

15. Meltzer, Bonnie. "Cheating the Kids." *Library Talk* 13, no. 2 (March/April 2000): 31-32.

16. Wombat image source: Anne Foxworthy's *Nature Gallery* (1996) [Online]. Available: http://www.cohsoft.com.au/nature/gallery/w/wombathn.jpg. (Used by permission).

17. Ibex image source: Amanda Ortega's page for the Fort Worth Zoo (June 2001) [Online]. Available: http://www.whozoo.org/Intro99/ortega/aortnubianibex.htm. (Used by permission).

18. Pink rose clip art image source: *AAA Internet Publishing* (2001) [Online]. Available: http://www.AAAInternet.com

19. Pink rose photo image source: taken by Lou Fournier (April 20, 2001) in Herb and Shan Jolly's garden, used with permission.

20. Meltzer, op. cit.

21. Steele, Bob. *Draw Me a Story: An Illustrated Exploration of Drawing-As-Language*. Winnipeg, Manitoba, Canada: Pegus Publishers, 1998, p. 3.

22. Eisner, Elliot, and Trela-Berger, Anne. "Looking at Art Through the MInd's Eye," *Stanford Educator*, Stanford University School of Education News, Spring 1996, pp. 2, 12.

23. Matthew Brady's photos of Civil War. Source of "Gettysburg hero" and over 1,000 other photos by Matthew Brady. *American Memory: Selected Civil War Photographs* (2001). [Online Archive]. Washington, DC: Library of Congress. Available: http://memory.loc.gov/ammem/cwphtml/cwhome.html

24. Juergen Mueller-Schneck's collection of photos of the Berlin wall. See actual photos of the Berlin Wall and its impact on both East and West German citizens during the Cold War in this vivid collection. *Web Photo Exhibition: The Berlin Wall* (2001).[Online Archive]. Available: http://www.dieberlinermauer.de/indexenglish.html

25. Alan Jacobs's photos of the Holocaust. The shocking, stark realism of these photos will leave its mark on the memories of anyone who views them. This Web site shows these photos, original artwork by survivors, and related information. *A Cybrary of the Holocaust: Remember.org*. (2001). [Online Articles and Archive]. Available: http://www.remember.org

Chapter 3

1. Will-Harris, Daniel "Choosing and Using Type." *Will-Harris House* (2001). [Online Article]. Available: http://www.will-harris.com/use-type.htm

2. Concept borrowed from an Adobe ad on the importance of fonts (circa 1995).

3. Veen, Greg. "Digital Images and the 'New' Visual Literacy." (January 2000). [Online Article]. Available: http://students.washington.edu/gveen/english/visual/conc2.html

4. Adobe, *Photoshop 6.0 User Guide* (p. 251). Adobe Press, 2001.

5. *Kinko's IMPRESS*, Issue 1/2000, Forbes' Special Interest Publications, New York, inside cover advertisement. (Used by permission).

6. Will-Harris, op. cit.

7. Ibid.

8. Haley, Allan. "Follow the Script." *Kinko's IMPRESS*, no. 5 (2001): 4–5.

9. Will-Harris, op. cit.

10. Ibid.

11. Williams, Robin, and John Tollet. *The Non-Designer's Web Book.* Berkeley, CA: Peach Pit Press, 1998, pp.110–111.

12. Will-Harris, op. cit.

13. "Type Resources." Adobe Web site (2001) [Online Article]. Available: http://www.adobe.com/type/topics/Info5.html

14. Ibid.

Chapter 4

1. Chudler, Eric H. "The Stroop Test," *Neuroscience for Kids.* Seattle: University of Washington (2001). [Online Article]. Available: http://faculty.washington.edu/chudler/words.html. (Used by permission).

2. "*Brand Packaging* magazine noted recently that 80% of a consumer's buying decision is based on color." Quoted in Kinko's *Impress* magazine (Issue 1/2000), p. 15.

3. Wagner, Carlton. *Color Power.* Chicago: Wagner Institute for Color Research, 1985, pp. 22, 37–38.

4. Ibid, pp. 25–26.

5. *American Memory: Selected Civil War Photographs* (2001). [Online Archive]. Washington, DC: Library of Congress. Available: http://memory.loc.gov/ammem/cwphtml/cwphome.html

6. Monet. *The Poppies.* (1873) [Online]. Available: http://www.ibiblio.org/wm/paint/auth/monet/first/monet.coquelicots.jpg

7. "Investigating the Effects of Color, Fonts, and Bold Text in Documents," Working Paper #WP0196.029, by investigative researchers Ellen D. Hoadley, Laurette Simmons, and Faith Gilroy, at the David D. Lattanze Center for Executive Studies in Information Systems, Loyola College, Baltimore, MD. (1995). [Online Article]. Available: http://www.accentcolor.com/products/wp0196.029.html

8. Walker, Morton. *The Power of Color.* New York: Avery Publishing Group, 1991, pp. 43–44.

9. Ibid., p. 44.

10. Graham, Helen. *Discover Color Therapy*, as reported in *InnerSelf* (January 1998) [Online Article]. Available: http://www.innerself.com/Magazine/Health/Color_Therapy_part_2.htm

11. Study conducted by Henner Ertel, Director of the Institute for Rational Psychology, Munich, Germany; see http://www.grp-net.com (in German). For a brief description of this study, see Alley Katt Designs, *Alley Katt's Place: All About Color* (2001). [Online Article]. Available: http://www.alleykatt.com/colors/

12. Wohlfarth, Harry, and Sam, Catherine. "The Effect of Color Psychodynamic Environmental Modification upon Psychophysiological and Behavioral Reactions of Severely Handicapped Children." *The International Journal of Biosocial Research* 3, no.1 (1982): 10–38.

13. See an explanation of sepia color on Brittanica.com. Search for "sepia" at http://www.britannica.com/

14. Caillebotte. *Rue de Paris, temps de pluie* (*Paris Street, Rainy Day*). (1877) [Online]. Available: http://www.ibiblio.org/wm/paint/auth caillebotte/rainy.jpg

van Gogh. *Olive Trees with Yellow Sky and Sun*. (1889) [Online]. Available: http://www.ibiblio.org/wm/paint/auth/gogh/fields/gogh.olive-trees.jpg

Monet. *Water Lilies*. (1906) [Online]. Available: http://www.ibiblio.org/wm/paint/auth/monet/waterlilies/monet.wl-1906.jpg

Rembrandt. *Philosopher in Meditation*. (1632) [Online]. Available: http://www.ibiblio.org/wm/paint/auth/rembrandt/1630/meditation.jpg

15. "Warm Colors." Sanford ArtEdventures (1999) [Online]. Available: http://www.sanford-artedventures.com/study/g_warm.html

16. Cezanne. *Chairback*. (1902–1906) [Online]. Available: http://www.ibiblio.org/wm/paint/auth/cezanne/sl/chairback/cezanne.chairback.jpg

van Gogh. *Vase with Twelve Sunflowers*. (1889) [Online]. Available: http://www.ibiblio.org/wm/paint/auth/gogh/sl/gogh.12-sunflowers.jpg

van Gogh. *Pollard Willows with Setting Sun*. (1888) [Online]. Available: http://www.ibiblio.org/wm/paint/auth/gogh/landscapes/gogh.willows.jpg

van Gogh. *Red Vineyard*. (1888) [Online]. Available: http://www.ibiblio.org/wm/paint/auth/gogh/vineyards/gogh.red-vineyard.jpg

Cezanne. *Lake Annecy*. (1896) [Online]. Available: http://www.ibiblio.org/wm/paint/auth/cezanne/land/lake-annecy.jpg

Caillebotte. *Rooftops Under Snow*. (1878) [Online]. Available: http://www.ibiblio.org/wm/paint/auth/caillebotte/baillebott.rooftops-snow.jpg

van Gogh. *The Starry Night*. (1889) [Online]. Available: http://www.ibiblio.org/wm/paint/auth/gogh/starry-night/gogh.starry-night.jpg

van Gogh. *Thatched Cottages at Cordeville*. (1890) [Online]. Available: http://www.ibiblio.org/wm/paint/auth/gogh/landscapes/gogh.cordeville.jpg

Matisse. *Notre Dame in the Late Afternoon*. (1902) [Online]. Available: http://www.ibiblio.org/wm/paint/auth/matisse/matisse.notre-dame-am.jpg

17. Osterink, Marcia. *Arts Attack—Art Training 4 Teachers and Creative Kids*, available from Marcia Osterink, 4615 Rancho Reposo, Del Mar, CA 92014 (phone: 1-888-760-ARTS (2787); e-mail: artsattk@utm.net).

18. See the chart about the meanings of color on this site: Lineback, Richard. *Color on the Web: Psychology of Colour*. (1998) [Online]. Available: http://members.tripod.com/Ranger_Ron/colour.htm

19. Wagner, Carlton. *Color Power*, p. 43.

20. Lineback, Richard. *Color on the Web: Cultural Differences*. (1998) [Online]. Available: http://members.tripod.com/Ranger_Ron/culture.htm

21. Van Eyck. *The Arnolfini Marriage*. (1434) [Online]. Available: http://www.ibiblio.org/wm/paint/auth/eyck/arnolfini/arnolfini.jpg

22. Rembrandt. *Saskia as Flora*. (1634) [Online]. Available: http://www.abcgallery.com/R/rembrandt/rembrandt65.html

23. Morton, J. L. *Color and Culture Matters*. (2001) [Online Article]. Available: http://www.colormatters.com/culturematters.html

24. Walker, Morton. *The Power of Color*, p. 45.

25. Botticelli. *Madonna of the Pomegranate*. (1487) [Online]. Available: http://www.ibiblio.org/wm/paint/auth/botticelli/botticelli.madonna-pomegranate.jpg

Lippi, Fra Filippo. *Annunciation*. (mid-1400s) [Online]. Available: http://sunsite.auc.dk/cgfa/lippi/p-lippi10.htm

Lippi, Fra Filippo. *Virgin in Adoration*. (mid-1400s) [Online]. Available: http://www.sanfordartedventures.com/play/color2/images/lippi_1.jpg

26. Sanford ArtEdventures. *Color Theory*. (1999) [Online].

Available: http://www.sanford-artedventures.com/play/color2/d2a.html

27. Wagner, Carlton. *Color Power*, p. 99.

28. Graham, Helen. "Discover Color Therapy." *InnerSelf* (2001) [Online]. Available: http://www.innerself.com/Magazine/Health/Color_Therapy_part_2.htm

29. Alley Katt Designs. *All About Color*. Dallas, TX: Author, 1997. [Online]. Available: http://www.alleykatt.com/colors/allcolor.htm

30. Wagner, Carlton. *Color Power*, pp. 103, 108–109.

31. Ibid., pp. 103, 110.

32. Ibid., p. 104.

33. Parker, Roger C., and Berry, Patrick. *Looking Good in Print*. Scottsdale, AZ: Creative Professionals Press, 1998.

34. Weinman, Lynda. *Deconstructing Web Graphics*. Indianapolis, IN: New Riders Publishing, 1996.

35. Alley Katt Designs, op. cit.

36. Suess, Dr. *My Many Colored Days*, illustrated by Steven Johnson and Lou Fancher. New York: Knopf, 1998.

37. Suess, Dr. *Suessville: My Many Colored Days*. (1999) [Online]. Available: http://www.randomhouse.com/seussville/titles/days/

38. Carle, Eric. *Hello, Red Fox*. New York: Simon & Schuster, 1998.

Jonas, Ann. *Round Trip*. New York: Greenwillow Press, 1983.

Walsh, Ellen Stoll. *Mouse Paint*. New York: Econo-Clad Books, 1999.

Chapter 5

1. Spear, William. *Feng Shui Made Easy*. San Francisco: Harper Collins Publishers, 1995, pp. 61–63.

2. Ibid., p. 63.

3. Feldman, Jean R. *Wonderful Rooms Where Children Can Bloom!* Peterborough, New Hampshire: Crystal Springs Books, 1997, pp. 124–126.

4. Ibid., p. 124.

5. Ibid., p. 125.

6. Dunitz, Robin J. *Street Gallery: Guide to over 1000 Los Angeles Murals*. Sherman Oaks, CA: R. J. D. Enterprises, 1998.

Dunitz, Robin J., and Prigoff, James. *Painting the Towns: Murals of California*. Sherman Oaks, CA: R. J. D. Enterprises, 1997.

7. *Bill of Rights mural*. (2001) [Online]. Available: http://www.lessonplanspage.com/SSBillOfRightsMuralIdea812.htm

8. Black, Kathy. *City Scapes*. (2001) [Online]. Available: http://homepage.mac.com/krohrer/iad/lessons/elem/elem14.html

9. *Table Murals*. (2001) [Online]. Available: http://homepage.mac.com/krohrer/iad/lessons/elem/elem9.html

10. Bolles, Richard Nelson. *What Color Is Your Parachute?* Berkeley, CA: Ten Speed Press, 2001.

11. Kinko's *IMPRESS* magazine, Forbes Special Interest Publications, Inc., New York, Issue 3/2000, inside cover. (Used by permission).

12. Rootham, Peter. *Macbeth Pie Chart*. Outta Ray's Head Literature site. (2001). [Online]. Available: http://www.cgocable.net/~rayser/litera1.htm#macplay\

13. Family Education Network. *Hamburger template*. (2001) [Online]. Available: http://www.familyeducation.com/printables/piece/0,2357,23-17455-1397,00.html

14. Bolles, Richard Nelson. *The What Color Is Your Parachute Workbook*. Berkeley, CA: Ten Speed Press, 1998.

15. *Metropolitan Museum of Art, Portrait Gallery*. (2001) [Online]. Available: http://www.metmuseum.org

16. *National Portrait Gallery, British Portraits Collection*. (2001) [Online]. Available: http://www.npg.org.uk

17. Sanford ArtEdventures. *Art Lessons on Portraits*. (1999) [Online]. Available: http://www.sanford-artedventures.com/teach/lp_portrait1_complete.html

18. Tompkins, Nancy. *Emotion Commotion.* (2001) [Online]. Available: http://homepage.mac.com/krohrer/iad/lessons/elem/elem1.html

19. *A Look at Self-Portraits for Students.* (2001) [Online]. Available: http://teachnet.com/lesson/art/selfportr092299.html

20. Feldman, op. cit., p. 13.

21. Ibid., p. 28.

Chapter 6

1. Ganzel, Rebecca. "Power Pointless," *Presentations* (February 2000): pp. 29–31. [Online]. Available: http://www.presentations.com/techno/soft/2000/02/29_f2_ppl.html

2. Page, Brian. "zionnp01.jpg," *Pics4Learning* (August 2000) [Online}. Available: http://pics.tech4learning.com

3. Simons, Tad. "A little magic can go a long way in this imperfect world." *Presentations* (February 1999) [Online]. Available: http://www.presentations.com/deliver/audience/1999/02/21_pod_alit.html

4. 3M Corporation research cited in "Polishing Your Presentation." *3M Meeting Network Articles & Advice* (2001) [Online Article]. Available: http://www.3m.com/meetingnetwork/readingroom/meetingguide_pres.html

5. Hanke, Jon. "How timing affects retention." *Presentations* (May 1998): 13. [Online Article]. Available: http://www.presentations.com/deliver/audience/1998/05/13_f1_psy_03.html

6. Waldrop, Dawn. "What you wear is almost as important as what you say." *Presentations* 14, no. 7 (July 2000): 74.

Chapter 7

1. Preston, Morag. "Slide Rules." *IMPRESS* 5 (2001): 47.

2. Hanke, op. cit., p. 49.

3. Endicott, Jim. "For the prepared presenter, fonts of inspiration abound." *Presentations* (April 1999): 26.

4. *The Brain Explorer.* (2001) [Online]. Available: http://www.exploratorium.edu/brain_explorer/index.html

5. Hanke, Jon. "Psychology of Presentation Visuals." *Presentations* (May 1998): 49.

6. Ibid.

7. Ibid., pp. 47–48.

8. Ibid., p. 47.

9. Holmes, Nigel. "The State of the Chart." *IMPRESS* 3 (2000): 6.

10. Ibid., pp. 6-7.

11. Endicott, Jim. "A strong template identity creates powerful impressions." *Presentations* (August 1999): 29–30.

12. Lindstrom, Robert L. "Meet your future: 13 ways presenting will change." *Presentations* (April 1998): 14.

Chapter 8

1. Jursic, Michael. "The Joke and the Paragraph." (2001). [Online]. Available: http://www.cgocable.net/ ~ rayser/joke.txt

2. Pics4Learning Home Page. (2001) (Online). Available: http://pics4learning.com

3. Danielle, Josh, Kelsy, Vanessa, and Chandra—students at Crescent Heights Elementary School.

4. Michael, student at Granada High School.

5. Jacobs, Alan. *Shoes.* (1980). [Online]. Available: http://www.remember.org

6. Insinnia, Elaine, Eileen Sharecki, Jarnail Tucker, and Rose Reissman. "Teach a Novel without the Internet? Never Again!" *Learning & Leading with Technology* (May 2000): 28–35.

7. *World War II Propaganda: Mobilizing Artists to Mobilize Others.* (2001). [Online]. Available: http://www.justthink.org/lessons/4wwII/wwII.html

8. National Archives. *Picturing the 20th Century* Exhibition. (2001) [Online].Available: http://www.nara.gov/exhall/ picturing_the_century/home.html

9. American Museum of Photography. (2001) [Online]. Available: http://www.photographymuseum.com

10. Richard, Stan. *Sun Pillar*. (March13, 2001)/ [Online]. Available: http://antwrp.gsfc.nasa.gov/apod/ap010313.html

11. NASA Education Web Site. (2001) [Online]. Available: http:// education.nasa.gov

12. *Flagler Museum*. (1995) [Online]. Available: http://www .flagler.org

Note: Along with John D. Rockefeller and Samuel Andrews, Henry Flagler founded Standard Oil in 1870. In his 50s, Flagler became interested in Florida and by his death, Flagler's Florida East Coast Railway linked the entire east coast of Florida, from Jacksonville to Key West, establishing agriculture and tourism as Florida's leading industries. In 1902, Flagler built the White-hall estate in West Palm Beach. Today, Whitehall is a National Historic Landmark and is open to the public as the Flagler Museum. The Museum has been featured in many television programs and magazine articles nationwide, as one of America's great Gilded Age Estates.

13. National Oceanic and Atmospheric Administration (NOAA). *NOAA Photo Gallery*. (2001) [Online]. Available: http://www .photolib.noaa.gov/collections.html. *Note:* Photos in this collec-tion are in the public domain and cannot be copyrighted. How-ever, credit should be given to the NOAA and the photographer, where specified.

14. National Oceanic and Atmospheric Administration (NOAA). *Beginnings and Endings: NOAA Photo Gallery*. (2000) [Online]. Available: http://www.photolib.noaa.gov/sun/index.html

15. King, Martin Luther Jr. *I Have a Dream*. (2000). [Online]. Available: http://web66.coled.umn.edu/new/MLK/MLK.html. *Note:* The speech was delivered on the steps of the Lincoln Memorial in Washington, D.C., on August 28, 1963. Full text posted here and on various other Web sites.

16. See the rubric for evaluating student writing on Jerome Burg's Web site: *Meet Jerome Burg*. (2000). [Online]. Available: http://homepage.mac.com/jburg/vitae/Index.html

Bibliography

Bolles, R. N. (1998). *The what color is your parachute workbook.* Berkeley, CA: Ten Speed Press.

Bolles, R. N. (2001). *What color is your parachute?* Berkeley, CA: Ten Speed Press.

Christopherson, J. T. (1996, October). The growing need for visual literacy at the university. In R. E. Griffin (Ed.), *VisionQuest: Journeys toward visual literacy* (pp. 169–174). Proceedings of the 28th International Visual Literacy Association Conference, Cheyenne, Wyoming.

Dunitz, R. J. (1998). *Street gallery: Guide to over 1000 Los Angeles murals.* Sherman Oaks, CA: R. J. D. Enterprises.

Dunitz, R. J., & Prigoff, J. (1997). *Painting the towns: Murals of California.* Sherman Oaks, CA: R. J. D. Enterprises.

Dunn, J. L. (1994, April). Television watchers. *Instructor,* pp. 50–54.

Eco, U. (1979). *A theory of semiotics.* Bloomington: Indiana University Press.

Edmark-Riverdeep Corporation. (2001). Millie & Bailey Kindergarten [software]. Redmond, WA: Author.

Eisner, E., & Trela-Berger, A. (1996, Spring). Looking at art through the mind's eye. *Stanford Educator News* (Stanford University School of Education), pp. 2, 12.

Endicott, J. (1999, April). For the prepared presenter, fonts of inspiration abound. *Presentations,* pp. 26–30.

Endicott, J. (1999, August). A strong template identity creates powerful impressions. *Presentations,* pp. 28–31.

Feldman, J. R. (1997). *Wonderful rooms where children can bloom!* Peterborough, NH: Crystal Springs Books.

Ganzel, R. (2000, February). Power pointless. *Presentations,* pp. 53–58.

Gardner, H. (1983). *Frames of mind.* New York: Basic Books.

Haley, A. (2001). Follow the script. *Kinko's IMPRESS* (Issue 5/2001). New York: Forbes' Special Interest Publications.

Hanke, J. (1998a, May). How timing affects retention. *Presentations,* p. 13.

Hanke, J. (1998b, May). The psychology of presentation visuals. *Presentations,* pp. 42–51.

Holmes, N. (2000). The state of the chart. *Kinko's IMPRESS* (Issue 3/2000, p. 6). New York: Forbes' Special Interest Publications.

Insinnia, E., Sharecki, E., Tucker, J., & Reissman, R. (2000, May). Teach a novel without the Internet? Never again! *Learning & Leading with Technology, 27*(8), 28–35.

Levie, W. H., & Lentz, R. (1982). Effects of text illustrations: A review of research, *Educational Communication and Technology Journal, 30*(4), 195–232.

Lindstrom, R. L. (1999, April 19). Being visual: The emerging visual enterprise. *Business Week* (Special Advertising Section).

Lindstrom, R. L. (1998, April). Meet your future: 13 ways presenting will change. *Presentations,* pp. 10–14.

Lindstrom, R. L. (2000, July 31). Visual communications @ work. *Business Week* (Special Advertising Supplement).

Meltzer, B. (2000, March/April). Cheating the kids. *Library Talk, 13*(2), 31–32.

Meredith, G. (1999, October).The demise of writing. *The Futurist, 33*(8), 27–29.

Parker, R. C., & Berry, P. (1998). *Looking good in print.* Scottsdale, AZ: Creative Professionals Press.

Pavio, A. (1986). *Mental representations: A dual coding approach.* New York: Oxford University Press.

Postman, N. (1993). *Technopoly: The surrender of culture to technology.* New York: Vintage Books.

Postman, N. (1996). *The end of education: Redefining the value of school.* New York: Knopf.

Preston, M. (2001). Slide rules. *IMPRESS* (Issue5/2001, pp. 47–49). New York: Forbes' Special Interest Publications, Inc.

Rakes, G. C. (1999, September). Teaching visual literacy in a multimedia age. *TechTrends, 43*(4), 14–18.

Seuss, Dr. (Theodor Seuss Geisel). (1998). *My many colored days* (S. Johnson & L. Fancher, illus.). New York: Knopf.

Simons, T. (1999, February). A little magic can go a long way in this imperfect world. *Presentations,* p. 21.

Simons, T. (2000, February). Multimedia or bust? (H. Andres & C. Peterson, researchers). *Presentations,* pp. 48–50.

Spear, W. (1995). *Feng Shui made easy.* San Francisco: Harper Collins.

Steele, B. (1998). *Draw me a story: An illustrated exploration of drawing-as-language.* Winnipeg, Manitoba, Canada: Pegasus Publishers.

Wagner, C. (1985). *Color power.* Chicago: Wagner Institute for Color Research.

Waldrop, D. (2000, July).What you wear is almost as important as what you say. *Presentations,* pp. 31–32.

Walker, M. (1991). *The power of color.* New York: Avery Publishing Group.

Weinman, L. (1996). *Deconstructing Web graphics.* Indianapolis, IN: New Riders Publishing.

Will-Harris, D. (2001). Choosing and using type. [Online article]. *Will-Harris graphic design.* Available: http://www.will-harris .com/use-type.htm

Williams, R., & Tollet, J. (1998). *The non-designer's Web book.* Berkeley, CA: Peach Pit Press.

Wohlfarth, H., & Sam, C. (1982). The effect of color psychodynamic environmental modification upon psychophysiological and behavioral reactions of severely handicapped children. *The International Journal of Biosocial Research, 3*(1), 10–38.

▌Index

▶ About the Author

Lynell Burmark is a distinguished pioneer in education, as a teacher—with years of classroom teaching experience in both K–12 and higher education—as an administrator, and as a professional speaker. Cofounder of VisionShift International, a nonprofit organization dedicated to advancing innovative new approaches to learning, she is also an Associate in the Thornburg Center for Professional Development.

Burmark holds two master's degrees and a Ph.D. from Stanford University and is in frequent demand as a speaker, trainer, writer, strategist, and consultant. Her ground-breaking multimedia workshop "Strategies for Successful Presentations" quickly established her as a leader in visual literacy and practical applications of its principles for powerful communications. As an education administrator, the author was recognized for her many creative accomplishments in multicultural understanding and use of technology in education.

Contact information for the author:

Lynell Burmark
Phone: (408) 733-0288
Fax: (408) 432-4316
Email: lynellb@aol.com

World Wide Web:
Thornburg Center: http://www.tcpd.org
VisionShift/National Heritage Foundation: http://www.nhf.org

Related ASCD Resources: Visual Learning

ASCD stock numbers are noted in parentheses.

Audiotapes

The Internet and Brain-Based Learning: A Powerful Team, by Kim Lindey and Kristen Nelson (#201128)

On Multiple Intelligences and Education by Howard Gardner (#295056)

Presentation Skills for Leaders (#200081) by Annette Segal

Networks

Visit the ASCD Web site (www.ascd.org) and search for "networks" for information about professional educators who have formed groups around topics like "Arts in Education," "Authentic Assessment," "Brain-Based Compatible Learning," and "Holocaust and Genocide Information." Look in the "Network Directory" for current facilitators' addresses and phone numbers.

Online Resources

Visit ASCD's Web site (www.ascd.org) for the following professional development opportunities and many others:

Online Tutorials (www.ascd.org/frametutorials.html): The Brain and Learning, Constructivism, Learning Styles, Multiple Intelligences, and others (free)

Professional Development Online: *Memory and Learning Strategies* by Marcia D'Arcangelo (www.ascd.org/framepdonline.html) (for a small fee; password protected)

Print Products

Activating and Engaging Habits of Mind (#100033) by Arthur L. Costa and Bena Kallick

Arts with the Brain in Mind (#101011) by Eric Jensen

ASCD Topic Packs: *Arts Education* (#197197); *Multiple Intelligences* (#198220)

Classroom Instruction That Works (#101010) by Robert J. Marzano, Debra J. Pickering, and Jane E. Pollock

Curriculum/Technology Quarterly (Spring 2001): Technology for the Visual and Performing Arts (#101054)

Design Tools for the Internet-Supported Classroom (#198009) by Judi Harris

Dimensions of Learning Teachers' Manual (2nd ed.) (#197133) by Robert J. Marzano, Debra Pickering, and others

Educational Leadership: Teaching the Information Generation (Vol. 58, No. 2, October 2000) (#100284)

A Field Guide to Using Visual Tools (#100023) by David Hyerle

In Search of Understanding: The Case for Constructivist Classrooms (rev. ed.) (#199234) by Jacqueline Grennon Brooks and Martin G. Brooks

Multiple Intelligences in the Classroom (2nd ed.) (#100041) by Thomas Armstrong

Understanding by Design (#198199) by Grant Wiggins and Jay McTighe

Using the Internet to Strengthen Curriculum (#100042) by Larry Lewin

Videotapes

The Brain and Learning (#498062), four tapes

How to Use Graphic Organizers to Promote Student Thinking (#499048), Tape 6 of the "How To" Series

The Multiple Intelligences Series (#495003) by Bruce and Linda Campbell

For additional information, visit us on the World Wide Web (http://www.ascd.org), send an e-mail message to member@ascd.org, call the ASCD Service Center (1-800-933-ASCD or 703-578-9600, then press 2), send a fax to 703-575-5400, or write to Information Services, ASCD, 1703 N. Beauregard St., Alexandria, VA 22311-1714 USA.